Praise for The

"Not since Berliner and Biddles's *A Manufactured Crisis* has there been such an expose' of the 'blame game' with respect to American schemes to identify and fix the schooling process. Bouie's brilliant chronology of save-face reform efforts is as insightful as it is transparent. From Sputnik to NCLB/RTTT, Bouie details the politically motivated knee-jerk attempts to fix the curriculum, the schools, the teachers to satisfy a demanding quest to appear superior to international powers. Buckle your seat belts because there is a crescendo that leads the reader to a vista of reason that clusters past mistakes of amiss reform efforts. By the time the reader is prepared for the whole truth, the suspense built for Chapter 10 is well worth the study time to unleash a laser focus to steer the ship of problem identification to safe shore of efficacy. This masterpiece should be required reading for the candidates of any Educator Preparation Program. Bouie's contribution will serve the field now and for years to come as a work of art, a work of superior journalism and a lesson in effective problem solving."

—Dr. Felicia Mitchell, Director, Clark Atlanta University

"Dr. Bouie has presented a very comprehensive history of modern day public education reform, beginning with the wake-up call of the launching of Sputnik and the National Defense Education Act (1958) to Every Student Succeeds Act (2015). It is logically presented and very informative. I found the section on "The Murky Role of the Federal Government" particularly compelling. Well Done!"

—Dr. Olivia Boggs, Associate Professor, Mercer University

"The Death of the Public School is a thought-provoking revelation of the genesis of public concern and non-traditional stakeholders growing fears and increased involvement in so called "School Reform". I was mesmerized as I read this book, having to relive the Sputnik moment that shook our nation's confidence to the core when Russian scientists launched the first satellite on Oct. 1st, 1957. The world took notice and America's position as the strongest nation was in jeopardy. At the end of the day, the spotlight shined on the American education system as the culprit that allowed such a thing to happen, and it's been that way ever since to define or defend all of America's ills. *We must fix public education* is the erroneous cry!

"The Death of the Public School, written by Dr. Wendolyn Bouie is a chilling expose of how we have politicized public education with mostly costly unworkable solutions that focus on everything except improving student's classroom performance and life achievements. It suggests that the real solution to student learning and achievement is to recognize and believe first that *all students can learn*, and that children being raised in poverty are just as bright as affluent students. They simply need to have their basic socioeconomic needs met and to know that we truly care about their well-being. Dr. Bouie writes that there is no Superman coming. There is no one size fits all. What works are family, school, and community partnerships working with master educators, parents and caring teachers. The educators identify the unique needs of each students, and together in partnership they provide the pedagogy, resources, and support, conducive to each student's academic and character success.

"The Death of the Public School is a must read, a powerful read—my good friend has done a masterful job. True to form she offers no silver bullet, however she does suggest you look at a couple of proven techniques, including her on that embody the concept that *All Kids Can Learn to High Expectations* when given the necessary love, discipline, resources, and support, *to make it happen!"*

—*Stanley Williams, Former US Dept. of Education Regional Representative, President of The Atlanta Committee for Public Education, and IBM Regional Executive*

"The Death of the Public School is a must read for governors, congressman, Board of Education superintendents and college professors. The theme of this mentally inspiring books is whether American schools are failing or is America failing to educate its children. *The Death of the Public School* presents a historical view of the misdirection of education in America beginning with the response to Sputnik and moving swiftly thorough *No Child Left Behind* to set the stage for how the crisis emerged, both educationally and politically. While renewed interest in continued restructuring through Standards Based Education is the new flavor the month, this book points out that many innovations actually engage in practices that marginally reflect the power of the original concept and therefore lacks sustainability of significant importance is the continued effort in to bring about innovations without truly identifying the problem and defining the purpose. Wendy Bouie does an exceptional job of integrating her practical experience with extensive research in providing a workable direction for education in America."

—Dr. Fannie Tartt, Retired Educator

"I've been in education for more than 40 years, as a teacher, parent, administrator, and board member. Never have I read such a comprehensive, practical, research-based book that provides an outline of the true picture of public schools as *The Death of the Public School*. This book provides hope for administrators to understand that spending time, energy, and funds on improving cognitive skills in low socio-economic areas without assisting with the affective areas. This book gives me hope that change will come in developing effective strategies for educating our students."

—Dr. Melvin Johnson, Chairman, Board of Education, DeKalb County Schools

THE DEATH OF THE PUBLIC SCHOOL

**Why so much money and good intentions
have failed our children's education
—and what to do about it**

By

Dr. Wendolyn Bouie

Printed in the United States of America
First Edition Printing

Design by
Arbor Services, Inc.
http://www.arborservices.co/

ISBN: 978-0-692-64701-1
LCCN: 2016902910

1. Title   2. Author   3. Education

Contents

PART ONE:
HOW WE GOT HERE

The Sputnik Moment

On a warm October evening in 1957, Lyndon B. Johnson, then majority leader of the United States Senate, was hosting one of his popular barbecue events at the LBJ Ranch in Texas. While busy attending to his guests he kept one ear on the news coming from the radio. There were persistent rumors that the Soviet Union was ready to launch the world's first satellite into Earth orbit, and he didn't want to miss it when it happened.

Late in the evening came the announcement from TASS, the official Soviet news agency. As published in *Pravda* the next day, the announcement said, in part, "On October 4, 1957, the first successful launch of the satellite was conducted in the USSR... The successful launch of the first human-made satellite of the Earth makes an enormous contribution into the treasury of the world science and culture. The scientific experiment conducted at such a high altitude has enormous importance for understanding of the properties of outer space and study of the Earth as a planet of our Solar system.

"In the course of the International geophysical year, Soviet Union expects to conduct launches of several more artificial satellites of the Earth. These follow-on satellites will have increased size and weight, and they will conduct a wide-range program of scientific research.

"Artificial satellites of the Earth will pave the way to interplanetary travel and, possibly, our contemporaries are destined to witness how freed and meaningful labor of the people of the new, socialist society makes a reality the most daring dreams of the humanity."

To a nation that had taken immense pride in its technological superiority, the news was electrifying. Like so many others, Johnson pondered the Soviet triumph. He remembered taking a walk, with eyes lifted skyward, straining to catch a glimpse of the tiny craft. "Now, somehow, in some new way, the sky seemed almost alien," he recalled. "I also remember the profound shock of realizing that it might be possible for another nation to achieve technological superiority over this great country of ours."

Like so many other Americans, Johnson resolved that something had to be *done* about this challenge. The nation had a problem, and the problem had to be fixed.

Returning to Washington, DC, at the end of November, Senator Johnson opened hearings by a subcommittee of the Senate Armed Services Committee to review the spectrum of American defense and space programs. This committee found significant underfunding and lack of organization for the conduct of space activities. Moving the issue straight into the arena of politics, it put the blame on President Eisenhower and the Republican Party. One of Johnson's aides, George E. Reedy, summarized the feelings of many Americans: "The simple fact is that we can no longer consider the Russians to be behind us in technology. It took them four years to catch up to our atomic bomb and nine months to catch up to our hydrogen bomb. Now we are trying to catch up to their satellite."

During the early years of the Cold War it was the Republicans that had been the opposition party. In 1949 Republicans had castigated President Harry S. Truman for the ouster of Chiang Kai-shek from mainland China and his replacement by a communist government under Mao Zedong, and again in 1950 for the invasion of South Korea to communist forces. Wisconsin Republican senator Joseph McCarthy had used these events to lambaste the Democrats as being soft on communism and of allowing the "Red Menace" to threaten the world. The Republicans had turned these issues into a political wave that had swept General Dwight D. Eisenhower into the presidency in 1952 along with a host of Republican members of Congress.

Now that the Republicans were in power, it was the turn of the Democrats to play the role of accuser and to demand action.

The Public Response: Do Something!

People respond to symbolic and easily understood events. And typically, if the event is perceived as a threat, the response is to demand *action*. With the Sputnik launches, the Soviet Union showed that it had mastered long-distance rocket technology and had the potential to send vehicles over our air space.

The skies over the continental United States had never been violated. During two world wars, not a single enemy aircraft had overflown America's mainland airspace. Suddenly, a craft launched by a hostile power was passing overhead. You could see it in the sky, and radio antennas could easily pick up its simple electronic beeps.

The bad news was easy to understand, and easy to respond to.

After the Sputnik moment, America's self-deprecation was boundless. America's editorial writers rushed to their typewriters, filling their pages with articles bemoaning the superficiality of much of US technical "progress."

Sputnik was launched on a Friday, and the following Monday CBS radio commentator Eric Sevareid began his broadcast:

"Here in the capitol, responsible men think and talk of little but the metal spheroid that now looms larger in the eye of the mind than the planet it circles around."

As author Paul Dickson related, a reporter for the *Washington Post*, Chalmers Roberts, wrote of the three things that were most on the minds of official Washington: "That Sputnik would have an extreme impact on the leaders of the underdeveloped world, who see it as a victory for socialism; that its surprising size and weight proved the Soviet Union had the power to launch and deliver an 'intercontinental ballistic missile with a multi-megaton hydrogen bomb warhead of several thousand pounds' to any point on the face of the Earth; and that a big argument was about to break out in Washington as to what must be done and who was responsible."

"What is at stake is nothing less than our survival," proclaimed Senator Mike Mansfield.

The Soviets will be "dropping bombs on us from space like kids dropping rocks onto cars from freeway overpasses," said Senator Lyndon Johnson.

"A severe blow—some would say a disastrous blow—has been struck at America's self-confidence and at her prestige in the world. Rarely have Americans questioned one another so intensely about our military position, our scientific stature, or our educational systems," intoned Senator Lister Hill.

Guessing what the Russians would do next became a national obsession. Speculation focused on the moon. One popular prediction held that the Russians might intend to mark the fortieth anniversary of their revolution on November 7, 1957, by sending an unmanned spacecraft to the moon and celebrating its arrival with the detonation of an atomic bomb.

In the battle for international influence, the Russian press seized the advantage. A *Pravda* dispatch from New York claimed that US senators were "showing signs of hysteria."

Foreign leaders began praising the Soviet Union and questioning the scientific ability of the United States. In the wake of Sputnik, Spain's Generalissimo Francisco Franco made unprecedented pro-Soviet and anti-American remarks.

Less than a week after the launch, Radio Cairo expressed the thoughts of many in the developing world: "The planetary era rings the death knell of colonialism. The American policy of encirclement of the Soviet Union has pitifully failed."

Our allies joined the chorus. The *Times of London* wrote of "the demon of inferiority which, since October 4, 1957... has disturbed American well-being."

A Gallup poll of seven foreign cities revealed that US prestige had eroded in six of them. Within weeks, there was a decline in public enthusiasm for "siding with the United States" and NATO in Germany, France, and Italy.

In Hong Kong, Japan, and the Philippines, there was a loss of confidence in the United States and a thinly veiled sense of glee that the Americans had been toppled from their high horse.

Thanks to the Sputnik moment, Wernher von Braun—a former Nazi rocket scientist—quickly became America's "space star." On October 29, 1957, von Braun gave a secret briefing to army officials in Washington, titled "The Lessons of Sputnik," in which he saw the event as a "national tragedy" that had done great damage to American prestige around the world. He went on to make two tough observations that made army officials uncomfortable.

The first was that the United States was committing a serious mistake in not being able to appraise the research and development capabilities of a nation that was run by a totalitarian regime, such as the Soviet Union.

He then pointed out how counterproductive and scattered the American military research and development had become. "About a year ago," he said, "I saw a compilation of all guided missile projects, which, at one time or another, had been activated in this country since 1945. I doubt if you will believe it, but the total figure was one hundred and nineteen different guided missile projects!"

Von Braun told the assembled group that while Americans understood the concept of teamwork when it came to football and baseball, the same did not apply to the serious business of rocket building.

To make matters worse, Sputnik soared overhead at a moment when America was anxious on several domestic fronts.

A seemingly robust economic boom had sputtered. Stock prices, which during the summer had started to sink, had been falling throughout the autumn. The Dow had dropped 21 percent in value since July 12, 1957, and the bull market that had been in place for more than three years was history. A recession was looming. Both personal and business incomes were down for the year, and unemployment was on the rise.

At the same time, social change was beginning to transform the United States. On September 9, 1957, less than a month before Sputnik's launch, the first civil rights legislation since

Reconstruction had been enacted in Congress. The 1957 Civil Rights Act was an attempt to ensure that all Americans could exercise their right to vote. Access to the ballot box was a big problem; in 1957, only about 20 percent of African Americans were registered to vote. Despite being a majority in numerous counties and congressional districts in the South, since the late nineteenth and early twentieth centuries most blacks had been locked out by discriminatory voter registration rules and laws that included literacy and comprehension tests, poll taxes, and other means.

Add to that the appearance of Sputnik, and it becomes clear why there was a sudden crisis of confidence not just in US technology but in our values and our ability to move ahead into a secure future.

President Dwight Eisenhower found himself in a difficult position. Being privy to inside information, he knew that we were not far behind the Russians, and that many secret US missile projects were underway. Indeed, the Jupiter-C rocket launched the first US satellite, Explorer I, four months after Sputnik 1.

Media commentators and politicians on Capitol Hill found President Eisenhower's response to Sputnik and his reassurances on the military significance of Sputnik inadequate. Democratic senator Stuart Symington declared that the president was "paternalistically vague." Walter Lippmann, perhaps the most influential columnist of the time, held that the president was "in a kind of partial retirement" and was letting the country drift and decline.

Regardless of the public perception of President Eisenhower's attitude, at the end of the day the consensus was to *do something* quickly; and the politically expedient approach was to focus on "fixing" the nation's schools.

The Solution: Fix Education

While Eisenhower did not share the public alarm about the launching of Sputnik, as a politician he knew he had to *take action*.

On October 10, 1057, six days after Sputnik's launch, there was a special meeting of the US National Security Council, held to address the implications of Sputnik for US security.

While alarmists publicly depicted Eisenhower as passive and unconcerned, he was fiercely dedicated to averting nuclear war at a time when the threat was very real. His concern for national security overruled the desire to beat the Russians into Earth orbit. The president, knowing far more about America's own satellite and ballistic missile research than he let on, refused to panic.

While Eisenhower was fully aware of the intensity of the public concern, and although he was a Republican and the former commander in chief of US forces in Europe during World War II, he did not want to respond to Sputnik by calling for a huge boost in military spending.

Thankfully, the answer seemed to lie elsewhere—specifically in education.

Just two weeks after Sputnik I, I. I. Rabi, chair of the president's Scientific Advisory Committee, warned that the emphasis on science and math in the Soviet education system would put the enemy ahead of the US in ten years.

Eisenhower called the training scientists and engineers "the most critical need of all... People are alarmed and thinking about science, and perhaps this alarm could be turned toward a constructive result."

He said the American people sho(
competition by investing in science and
He created a White House Office of Science a..
by the president of the Massachusetts Institute of Tecнил.
launched the National Aeronautics and Space Agency (NASA);
quintupled funding for the National Science Foundation; and
proposed increased federal, state, and local spending on education.

Indeed, the success of Sputnik inspired members of the
public to take an interest in elementary physics. Schoolteachers,
reporters, and editorialists found themselves dusting off textbooks
about the theories and laws of Sir Isaac Newton, who, almost
three centuries years earlier, had been the first one to theorize
how a satellite could work.

Science, including tradition-shaking theories, quickly
became more acceptable. Until late 1957, Charles Darwin and
his 1859 theory of evolution had been successfully kept out of
many classrooms. Only when Sputnik panicked the scientific
establishment did the theory of evolution find a place in high
school biology textbooks.

Schools began to place new emphasis on the process of
inquiry, independent thinking, and the challenging of long-held
assumptions. Laboratory science was stressed, urging a hands-on
learning approach. As useful as these measures may have been
in a limited context, they sprang from the stubborn and easy-
to-grasp belief that if only our schools were "better," we'd see
improvement in all students. The underlying problems were not
identified or addressed. They were the medical equivalent of a
placebo: the patient might feel as though they were being treated,
but in reality all they were getting was a sugar pill.

Dr. Wendolyn Bouie

Progressive vs. Fundamental Education

While the Sputnik moment provided sharp questions about the effectiveness and purpose of education, it was not the first time that education had been the subject of popular debate. Indeed, since time immemorial humans have taken sides about what education means and how to measure its effectiveness. While education reform may have its moments of higher visibility, it's never completely off the public radar screen. Schools are perennially subject to criticism.

For example, for nearly a century tension had existed between those who advocated for traditional education and those who advocated for progressive education. In the late 1800s traditionalist critics said that students were being "spoon-fed," the curriculum was too easy, and music and art took too much time from fundamentals.

Early practitioners of progressive education in the United States included Francis Parker and the philosopher John Dewey. In 1875 Francis Parker became superintendent of schools in Quincy, Massachusetts. Opposed to rote learning, and believing that there was no value in knowledge without understanding, he argued that schools should encourage and respect the child's creativity. Parker's Quincy System called for child-centered and experience-based learning. He replaced the traditional curriculum with integrated learning units based on core themes related to the knowledge of different disciplines. Traditional readers, spellers, and grammar books were replaced with children's own writing, literature, and teacher-prepared materials.

In 1896, John Dewey opened the University of Chicago Laboratory School, which intended "to discover in administration, selection of subject-matter, methods of learning, teaching, and discipline, how a school could become a cooperative community while developing in individuals their own capacities and satisfy their own needs." For Dewey the two key goals of developing a cooperative community and developing individuals' own capacities were necessary to each other.

In the twentieth century in America, the debate typically ranged around two areas of concern: *Who* should get educated, and *what* they should be taught.

Should everyone get a liberal arts education, or should members of lower economic classes get vocational training?

Should we spend as much in the cities as we can in the suburbs?

Should students learn applied science at the expense of cutting art classes?

The battle raged well into the postwar era. The Second World War had ended only ten years before Sputnik, and peacetime had spurred educational concerns that were largely demographic. In the postwar reform movement, the nation's colleges needed to accommodate returning veterans in numbers that had not been experienced before; and then within a few years the nation's elementary schools needed to do the same for the young baby boomers. The question was how to get more people educated.

In 1953, Albert Lynd published *Quackery in the Public Schools*. As a former professor, Lynd attacked progressivism and presented evidence on the lowering of learning and literacy in schools where the "real needs" curriculum had displaced the fundamentals, and an "activity" program of "room care and household pets" prevailed over arithmetic ("distasteful medicine"). *Kirkus Reviews* called the book "a stimulating, combative, cogent critique of the debasement of teaching and learning achievement in this country."

In *Educational Wastelands* (1953), Arthur Eugene Bestor Jr. charged that professional educationists had "lowered the aims of the American public schools," particularly by "setting forth purposes for education so trivial as to forfeit the respect of thoughtful men, and by deliberately divorcing the schools from the disciplines of science and scholarship." For Bestor, the traditional liberal arts curriculum represented the only acceptable form of secondary education. He charged that progressive educators, "by misrepresenting and undervaluing liberal education, have contributed... to the growth of anti-intellectualist hysteria that threatens not merely the schools but freedom itself."

On the progressive side, Rudolf Flesch's *Why Johnny Can't Read*, published in 1955, was a critique of the accepted practice of teaching reading by sight, often called the "look-say" method. The shortcoming of this method, according to Flesch, was that it required rote memorization with no theory supporting it. When confronted with an unknown word, the reader had nothing to draw upon. As a solution, Flesch advocated a revival of the phonics method, the teaching of reading by teaching learners to sound out words using rules. The book inspired Dr. Seuss to write *The Cat in the Hat*.

In the pre-Sputnik, postwar era, debate about the quality of American education raged. Individuals such as Admiral Hyman Rickover, and most notably Arthur Bestor, became critics of John Dewey's ideas and the rhetoric of progressive education, especially the theme of life adjustment.

The dominant theme of the critics was back to basics, back to fundamentals, back to drill and memorization, and back to facts.

While widespread public attention may only surface in response to a proclaimed crisis, efforts to change education rarely disappear altogether for any length of time. Dissatisfaction with schools not only waxes and wanes, it is sometimes general and sometimes local, and it is often domain specific, with reading and mathematics heading the list. It usually takes a crisis to mobilize nationwide action. But while the crisis occupies stage center, behind the scenes a set of persistent issues has been the focus of the reform struggles in this century. The Sputnik moment created concerns over the nation's curriculum, focusing not on *who* was being taught but *what* was being taught and how. In the case of science education, several key issues came to the forefront:

Who should decide what students are supposed to learn: the school community (parents, teachers, school administrators, and trustees) or education academics?

Which should have precedence in the schools: traditional, discipline-centered education or progressive, child-centered education?

How can we strike the balance between the stability that comes with maintaining traditional practices and content versus the uncertainty that comes with the introduction of major changes?

In the fall of 1957, the debate about American education reached a turning point. Sputnik resolved the debate in favor of those who advocated for greater emphasis on higher academic standards, with a renewed focus on science and mathematics. Sputnik convinced the American public that it was in the national interest to change education, in particular the curriculum in mathematics and science.

Although many had previously opposed federal aid to schools on the grounds that federal aid would lead to federal control, public opinion increasingly recognized that the effort needed to be made on the national level.

Curriculum reformers of the Sputnik era shared a common vision. Within the educational community and across disciplines, reformers sought to advance a curriculum based on the conceptually fundamental modes and ideas of mathematical problem solving and scientific inquiry. Reformers would supplement textbooks with instructional materials that included activities, films, and readings. The schools' traditional focus on science and mathematics programs emphasizing information, terms, and applied aspects of content would be transformed into the learning of structures and procedures of science and mathematics disciplines.

In the early 1950s, the nation did not exactly have a climate where progressive ideas could be calmly discussed. According to people like Senator Joseph McCarthy, you were either an American or you were a Commie—there was no middle ground. Educators often did not respond to their critics because they may have been fearful to defend progressive education, which by many accounts was on the decline. In 1955 the Progressive Education Association closed its doors, and two years later the journal *Progressive Education* folded. Those inclined to counter the critics may have thought their protests would make no difference.

Progressive educators had introduced the term "life adjustment" to describe programs for secondary schools that built on the "important needs of youth" expressed in the Educational Policy Commission's report, *Education for All American Children*, published in 1951. Life-adjustment education focused on the needs of students in "general tracks" and proposed a curriculum of functional experiences in areas such as family living, the practical arts, and civic participation. With the problem of Sputnik looming over the nation, progressive life-adjustment education did not convey a message that students would learn basic concepts of mathematics, science, and other disciplines. Progressive rhetoric about the curriculum seemed to neglect the real-life challenges that critics thought needed to be met.

Critics appealed to basic themes such as "restoration of learning," which implied students were not learning anything. The ideas and recommendations of critics were aligned with the educational experiences most adults had when they were in school and represented activities parents knew and could do with their children.

Sputnik I was never designed to stay in orbit indefinitely. In January 1958, the little gleaming sphere fell to earth. On this occasion, Gabriel Heatter, an influential news commentator for the Mutual Broadcasting System, delivered a radio editorial entitled "Thank You, Mr. Sputnik."

Addressing the deceased satellite, he said, "You will never know how big a noise you made. You gave us a shock which hit many people as hard as Pearl Harbor. You hit our pride a frightful blow. You suddenly made us realize that we are not the best in everything.

"You reminded us of an old-fashioned American word— humility. You woke us up out of a long sleep. You made us realize a nation can talk too much, too long, too hard about money.

"A nation, like a man, can grow soft and complacent. It can fall behind when it thinks it is Number One in everything. Comrade Sputnik, you taught us more about the Russians in one hour than we had learned in forty years."

Perhaps due to political and social divisions within the nation, moving beyond the "do something" reaction was not going to happen. Year after year, it was politically easy to rally the nation around a perceived common threat (Sputnik ably served in this role over and over again) and easy to pump federal dollars into the nation's schools to "fix" them. Looking deeper into the problem was perhaps too painful and too volatile, and so the federal doctor continued to prescribe placebos for a nation in need.

The National Defense Education Act of 1958

During the aftermath of the Second World War, among American educators and politicians the debate continued over what subjects schools should be teaching their students.

The progressive life adjustment movement was ascendant. The movement strove to provide a curriculum that would provide life skills that would be valuable for students who did not plan to continue on to college or other types of postsecondary training after high school. Spearheaded by the vocational educator Charles Prosser, this movement claimed to represent true democracy in education.

Many academicians criticized the life adjustment movement as being "soft." The National Science Foundation and other groups held schools of education and education professors responsible for what they asserted was the low achievement of American students, particularly in mathematics, science, and modern foreign languages.

With the launching of Sputnik I on October 4, 1957, the criticism of American education, especially its public schools, rose to a fever pitch. During the preceding years of the Cold War, Americans had felt protected by their technological superiority.

Suddenly the nation found itself lagging behind the Russians in the space race, and Americans worried that their system of education was not producing enough scientists and engineers. For the nation to meet the challenge, politicians, the media, and the public demanded *action*.

In a parallel development that increased the public's anxiety, in 1957 the United States was beginning to experience an acute shortage of mathematicians. The new electronic computer industry had created a demand for mathematicians as programmers. It also shortened the lead time between the development of a new mathematical theory and its practical application, thereby making the work of mathematicians more valuable. Industry, including defense, was absorbing the mathematicians who normally would have been academics working at high schools and universities to train the next generation. The postwar flood of European refugees had dwindled, so the nation had to increase the domestic supply.

Additionally, more high school graduates were beginning to attend college. In 1940 about one-half million Americans attended college, which was about 15 percent of their age group. By 1960, however, college enrollments had expanded to 3.6 million.

Because it was politically impossible for the federal government to insert itself directly into the issue of curriculum— that was strictly the purview of state and local government—the solution from Washington focused on education funding and access. In other words, making the existing system easier to enter.

On the day Sputnik first orbited the earth, the chief clerk of the Senate's Education and Labor Committee, Stewart McClure, sent a memo to his chairman, Alabama Democrat Lister Hill, reminding him that while during the last three sessions of Congress the Senate had passed legislation for federal funding of education, all of the bills had died in the House. McClure suggested that if they called the education bill a "defense bill," conservatives might accept it and the House might pass it. Senator Hill—a former Democratic whip and a savvy legislative tactician—seized upon on the idea.

While there had long been resistance to federal aid or involvement in education, public opinion now demanded government action, and the Senate once again moved ahead with its education bill. Knowing that such a bill had plenty of opponents in the House, Senator Hill enlisted the aid of another Alabama Democrat, Representative Carl Elliott, who chaired the House subcommittee on education. At a meeting in Montgomery, they developed a strategy for passing legislation. Opponents in the House had always denounced the idea of federal student grants as "socialist." Senator Lister and Representative Elliott framed the debate around the question of whether federal funds should go to students as *grants*, as the Senate preferred, or as *loans*, which might be palatable to the more conservative House. Senator Hill and Representative Elliott surmised that having voted the same bill down repeatedly in the past, the House had to have something it could call a victory.

When the House prevailed and made federal assistance available only in the form of loans, the rest of the Senate's version of the bill sailed through.

To help gain acceptance of the fact that the bill made education a concern of the federal government, in his message to Congress on January 27, 1958, President Dwight Eisenhower called for the improved alignment of education with national defense needs and recommended the federal government play an important part in this mission.

Who could argue with the impulse to strengthen our national defense, even if this was a backdoor way to exert more federal control over the mottled patchwork of state, county, and city education districts?

Supporters of what was being called the National Defense Education Act (NDEA) pointed to federal legislative precedents.

In 1862, the Morrill Act had granted land to the states that they could then sell to finance the establishment of colleges.

In 1917, the Smith-Hughes Act had funded vocational agricultural education programs.

Advocates of the NDEA contended that they were not interfering with the principle, long cherished by local politicians, that states and communities were responsible for the conduct of American schooling and institutions of higher education.

Opponents of the NDEA maintained that the proposed aid would unduly influence local educational policy and would give the federal government too much authority.

Other critics, such as the National Education Association and the Council of Chief State School Officers, objected to what in their perception was the narrow focus of the NDEA on science and technology, as well as the act's reliance for direction on the National Science Foundation's university-oriented community as opposed to the broader approach of the education-oriented US Department of Education.

The NDEA Becomes Law

In spite of such opposition, in September 1958 the National Defense Education Act was passed by Congress and signed into law by President Eisenhower. The NDEA was one of a suite of science initiatives inaugurated by President Eisenhower in 1958 with the goal to increase the technological sophistication and power of the United States.

The purpose of the NDEA was to improve and strengthen all levels of the American school system and to encourage students to continue their education beyond high school. Specific provisions included:

Title I served as an introduction to the content and purposes of the act. It reads in part, "The Congress hereby finds and declares that the security of the Nation requires the fullest development of the mental resources and technical skills of its young men and women. The present emergency demands that additional and more adequate educational opportunities be made available. The defense of this Nation depends upon the mastery of modern techniques developed from complex scientific principles. It depends as well upon the discovery and development of new principles, new techniques, and new knowledge."

Title II dealt with student loans, allocating the amounts and specifying how it would be divided among states. Initially, Title II provided scholarships (also known as grants) rather than loans. However, since congressmen were worried about the message sent by giving students a "free ride," the amount of scholarship money was reduced by the Senate, eliminated entirely by the House, and ultimately changed to an exclusively loan-based system before the act passed.

Title III authorized $70 million per year of the NDEA's four-year duration to strengthen science, math, and foreign language education. Latin and Greek programs are not funded under this title, on the grounds that they are not modern foreign languages, and thus do not support defense needs.

Title IV established a national fellowship program to be awarded for graduate education, with some of the money earmarked for those interested in becoming college professors. Certain fields, such as folklore, were specifically exempted from these fellowships. Title IV was also one of the only two federal programs (along with Title VI of the NDEA) in existence at the time that gave any funding to the humanities.

Title V authorized funding to train guidance counselors and to implement standardized testing programs that would identify "gifted and talented" students. This laid the groundwork for academically gifted (AG) and gifted & talented (GT) programs, and began the trend of using standardized testing in schools to measure competency.

Title VI authorized funding for Language Area Centers and Language Institutes. "Area studies" includes such subjects as African American studies and Latin American studies.

Title VII authorized funding for both the research and implementation of new education technologies, including radio, TV, film, and even teaching machines.

Title VIII provided funding for vocational training.

Title IX established the Science Information Institute and Science Information Council, operating under the National Science Foundation, to advise the government on technical issues.

Title X provided grants to the states for improving data collection and statistical analysis by state education agencies, as well as miscellaneous provisions regarding legal and pragmatic details of the act.

The NDEA included one leftover from the waning era of McCarthyism: Title X, Section 1001(f) was a mandate that all beneficiaries must sign an affidavit disclaiming advocacy of the overthrow of the US government. This silly loyalty oath provoked concern and protest from the American Association of University Professors and over one hundred and fifty educational institutions, who said it attempted to control beliefs and as such violated academic freedom. Initially, a small number of institutions including Barnard, Yale, and Princeton refused to accept funding under the student loan program established by the act because of the affidavit requirement.

After four years of quiet but constant protest, the disclaimer requirement was repealed in the fall of 1962 by President John F. Kennedy.

Meanwhile, A Nation Is Still Divided

On its face, the National Defense Education Act of 1958 became a successful legislative initiative in higher education. There are many provisions in the NDEA that have had a lingering impact on education policy and politics, including the legitimization of education technology, the push for standardized testing, and perhaps most significantly, the introduction of federal funding for schools and for education initiatives.

But it was a perceived external threat to the cultural and technological supremacy of the United States—the launch of Sputnik—that had propelled the efforts to pass the legislation. It was never the goal of NDEA to deeply reform the many inequities in the American education system. The fact remains that despite all the testing and technology and funding, education did not transcend the knee-jerk crisis response of "do something."

Then and now, the drive to meet a perceived threat has consistently deflected attention from the structural failings of the nation's school systems.

It's worth remembering that during the time of the introduction of NDEA, America's public institutions—her schools, restaurants, retail stores, barbershops, and bus lines—were largely segregated. It's true that some progress had been made, at least in the courts. In 1954, in a unanimous opinion, the US Supreme Court ruled in Brown v. Board of Education that separate schools were "inherently unequal." However, the court delayed deciding on how to implement the decision and asked for another round of arguments. That same year, in Bolling v. Sharpe, the court ruled that the federal government was under the same duty as the states and must desegregate the Washington, DC, schools.

The following year, in Brown II, the Supreme Court ordered the lower federal courts to require desegregation "with all deliberate speed."

Nevertheless, segregation and inequality persisted.

In 1959—a year after NDEA had become law—twenty-five thousand young people marched in Washington, DC, in support of integration. Meanwhile, school officials in Prince Edward County, Virginia, closed their public schools rather than integrate them. White students attended private academies; black students did not return to class until 1963, when the Ford Foundation funded private black schools. In 1964, the US Supreme Court ordered the county to reopen its schools on a desegregated basis.

In 1962, the Supreme Court ordered the University of Mississippi to admit James Meredith, an African American student. When Meredith arrived at Ole Miss to register for classes in September, he found the entrance blocked. Rioting erupted, and Attorney General Robert Kennedy sent five hundred US marshals to the school. Additionally, President John F. Kennedy sent military police, troops from the Mississippi National Guard, and officials from the US Border Patrol. When the riots and the standoff finally ended, on October 1, 1962, James Meredith became the first black student to enroll at the University of Mississippi. The following year, two African American students, Vivian Malone and James A. Hood, successfully registered at the University of Alabama despite Governor George Wallace's "stand in the schoolhouse door"—but only after President Kennedy federalized the Alabama National Guard.

The Civil Rights Act of 1964 addressed critical issues in education. Title IV of the act authorized the federal government to file school desegregation cases. Title VI of the act prohibited discrimination in programs and activities, including schools, receiving federal financial assistance.

And by the way, just as President Eisenhower had known would happen—but could not reveal to the public—the United States soon surpassed the Soviet Union in space exploration. While in April 1961 the nation suffered another shock when Soviet cosmonaut Yuri Gagarin became the first man to orbit the Earth, President Kennedy responded with his speech before Congress in which he discussed "urgent national needs." He asked for an additional seven to nine billion dollars over the next five years for the space program, proclaiming that "this nation should commit itself to achieving the goal, before the decade is out, of landing a man on the moon and returning him safely to the earth." Within a year, Alan Shepard and Gus Grissom became the first two Americans to travel into space. On February 20, 1962, John Glenn Jr. became the first American to orbit Earth. As space exploration continued through the 1960s, the United States was on its way to the moon. On July 20, 1969, the Apollo 11 astronauts—Neil Armstrong, Michael Collins, and Edwin "Buzz" Aldrin Jr.—realized President Kennedy's dream. Meanwhile, the Soviets focused on somewhat less glamorous but perhaps more useful space stations; the first space station ever put into orbit was Salyut 1, which was launched by the Soviet Union on April 19, 1971.

Did America's eventual success in space have any relation to NDEA? It's impossible to say.

Was American education transformed by NDEA? No; the law was a "do something" response to an easily understood challenge. It did little to address the serious structural issues that were deeply ingrained in the system.

As had happened so many times before, the nation's education doctor had examined the patient, declared the patient to be very ill, and then prescribed an expensive sugar pill. It's no wonder that year after year, the patient continued to suffer because the real disease was never diagnosed.

The Elementary and
Secondary Education Act of 1965

Just as the Sputnik launch was a clarion call to action in 1957, the growing awareness of poverty in America provided the next call to action in 1965.

Of course, there had always been poor people living in America. The real difference in the 1960s was that for the first time the very idea of "poverty" could be measured statistically, written about by scholars, and debated by politicians. The 1962 publication of Michael Harrington's *The Other America*, which revealed that poverty in America was far more prevalent than middle-class people had assumed, focused public debate on the issue, as did Dwight MacDonald's subsequent review of the book in *The New Yorker*. Many historians credit Harrington and the book, which John F. Kennedy purportedly read while president, with spurring Kennedy and then Johnson to formulate an antipoverty agenda.

The civil rights movement also brought the issue to the forefront. Groups like the NAACP and the Urban League were prominent allies of the Johnson administration in its push for the Economic Opportunity Act and other legislation on the topic.

After Kennedy's assassination, President Johnson decided to respond to civil rights pressures and religious conflicts over education by linking educational legislation to what he called his "War on Poverty."

In his State of the Union address on January 8, 1964, President Lyndon Johnson declared "War on Poverty." He said, "Our aim is not only to relieve the symptoms of poverty, but to cure it and, above all, to prevent it."

The effort centered around four pieces of legislation:

- The Food Stamp Act of 1964, which made the provisional food stamp program permanent.
- The Social Security Amendments of 1965, which created Medicare and Medicaid and also expanded Social Security benefits for retirees, widows, the disabled, and college-aged students.
- The Economic Opportunity Act of 1964, which established the Job Corps, the VISTA program, the federal work-study program, and a number of other initiatives.
- The Elementary and Secondary Education Act (ESEA), which Johnson signed into law on April 9, 1965. It was the most expansive federal education bill ever passed and constituted the most important educational component of the War on Poverty launched by the president.

As a former teacher, Johnson sincerely believed that equal access to education was vital to a child's ability to lead a productive life, and he wanted to find a way to put the power of the federal government behind the challenge. In a 1964 memo to the president, Commissioner of Education Francis Keppel had outlined three options for funneling federal dollars into the nation's education system:

The first was to provide general aid to public schools, but he pointed out that this could generate a negative reaction from Catholic schools.

The second was to provide general aid to both public and private schools, but this would create a negative reaction from the National Education Association (NEA) and large sectors of the Democratic Party who objected to federal aid to religious schools.

The third option, the one that eventually was followed, was to skip the idea of general aid and emphasize the educational aid to *poor* children, because this could attract the support of most groups.

Through a special source of funding described in Title I, ESEA allocated large resources to meet the needs of educationally deprived children, especially through compensatory programs for the poor. Section A of Title I provides grants to states to distribute directly to school districts. This has been, and still is, by far the largest source of federal money for local schools.

The preamble to Title I offered this mission statement:

"The Congress declares it to be the policy of the United States that a high-quality education for all individuals and a fair and equal opportunity to obtain that education are a societal good, are a moral imperative, and improve the life of every individual, because the quality of our lives ultimately depends on the quality of the lives of others."

The strategy to reach this goal was built around the idea of providing compensatory measures for agencies in low-income areas.

The act read, in part, "In recognition of the special educational needs of low-income families and the impact that concentrations of low-income families have on the ability of local educational agencies to support adequate educational programs, the Congress hereby declares it to be the policy of the United States to provide financial assistance... to local educational agencies serving areas with concentrations of children from low-income families to expand and improve their educational programs by various means (including preschool programs) which contribute to meeting the special educational needs of educationally deprived children" (Section 201, ESEA, 1965).

Following the enactment of the bill, Johnson stated that Congress had finally taken the most significant step of that century to provide help to all schoolchildren. He argued that the school bill was wide reaching, because "it will offer new hope to tens of thousands of youngsters who need attention before they ever enroll in the first grade," and will help "five million children of poor families overcome their greatest barrier to progress: poverty."

ESEA was developed under the principle of redress, which established that children from low-income homes required more educational services than children from affluent homes. As part of the act, Title I funding allocated one billion dollars a year to schools with a high concentration of low-income children. President Johnson asserted that ESEA would provide a handsome return on investment: "For every one of the billion dollars that we spend on this program, will come back tenfold as school dropouts change to school graduates."

ESEA had at least three major consequences for future legislative action.

First, it addressed the religious conflict by linking federal aid to educational programs directly benefiting poor children in parochial schools, and not the institutions in which they enrolled. Second, it signaled the switch from general federal aid to education toward categorical aid, and the tying of federal aid to national policy concerns such as poverty, defense, or economic growth. Third, to avoid criticisms of federal control over education, individual state departments of education were given the task of administering federal funds, which resulted in an expansion of state bureaucracies and larger involvement of state governments in educational decision making.

In 1968, ESEA was amended with Title VII, resulting in the Bilingual Education Act, which offered federal aid to local school districts to assist them to address the needs of children with limited English-speaking ability.

Prior to ESEA becoming law, the federal government had little involvement in education, leaving it as a state and local matter. This act changed that, and despite provisions against a national curriculum, set national standards for achievement. This did not account for the time it would take impoverished and low-achieving schools to catch up with their peers.

ESEA sparked a huge increase in federal education spending and regulations. The legislation's Title I was supposed to provide aid to K–12 schools in high-poverty areas, but by the end of the 1960s it was providing aid to 60 percent of the nation's school districts. Today, Title I is the largest federal subsidy program for K–12 education.

In addition to Title I, ESEA created subsidies for teacher training, educational research, school libraries, textbooks, student literacy, school technology, school safety, and other items. It also strengthened state-level school bureaucracies directly with "grants to strengthen state departments of education."

This was the first attempt to address cognitive issues through affective and cognitive solutions. Students with disabilities have benefited greatly from the Elementary and Secondary Education Act (ESEA) because the law requires their academic achievement to be measured and reported. As a result, more students with disabilities have been afforded the opportunity to learn and master grade level academic content.

Did it make a difference? Many commentators think not. Here's what Curtis L. Decker, executive director of the National Disability Rights Network, wrote in September 2015 in the *Huffington Post*:

"Forty years later, it is clear that the original intent of the ESEA has still not been met for too many children, especially children with disabilities. Indeed, according to the US Census Bureau, in 2014 the poverty rate for adults with disabilities was 28.7% as opposed to 13.6% for non-disabled adults. It is imperative that we demand that all children, including those with disabilities, be given access to a high quality education in order to fulfill the original intent of ESEA. To do otherwise would subject people with disabilities to a life of poverty and dependency."

Responses to ESEA

Naturally, with the enactment of ESEA, people wanted to know how educational progress could be measured, and whether the billions of federal dollars poured into state coffers actually boosted student achievement.

Professor James Coleman and others at Johns Hopkins University were commissioned by US Commissioner of Education Harold Howe to conduct a major study of a question that a lot of people were asking: given the choice between compensatory education (namely, ESEA) and simple racial integration, which strategy was more likely to equalize educational opportunities for poor minority students?

Coleman's federally funded analysis, titled "The Equality of Educational Opportunity" (EEOS), was published in 1966. The EEOS consisted of test scores and questionnaire responses obtained from first-, third-, sixth-, ninth-, and twelfth-grade students, and questionnaire responses from teachers and principals.

Coleman's report asserted that compensatory education— whether offered in racially integrated or in racially segregated schools—was unlikely to improve achievement levels. The report stated, "Differences in school facilities and curricula, which are made to improve schools, are so little related to differences in achievement levels of students that, with few exceptions, their efforts [or the effects of different classes or curricula] fail to appear in a survey of this magnitude."

The report also concluded that racial integration alone did little to boost academic achievement in urban schools. "Our interpretation of the data," Coleman wrote, "is that racial integration *per se* is unrelated to achievement insofar as the data can show a relationship."

Several studies done at Harvard as part of a reanalysis of Coleman's data reached similar conclusions, suggesting that the best way to improve academic achievement was neither with integration nor compensatory programs alone but, rather, to *raise overall family income.* A report by sociologist David Armor found that "programs which stress financial aid to disadvantaged black families may be just [as] important, if not more so, than programs aimed at integrating blacks into white neighborhoods and schools."

A separate study concluded that the "racial composition of the school... does not have a substantial effect [on academic achievement]—not nearly so strong as the social class composition of the school."

These and other studies found that when it came to improving academic achievement in the inner city, what mattered most was neither special programs nor racial integration but, rather, family background and socioeconomic status. Even though this conclusion became more accepted over time, policies at the state and federal level persistently focused on narrow school-based reforms—the impulse to *do something to our schools to make them better.* It's the same impulse that Sputnik ignited: if we make our schools better, we'll produce better scientists.

In 1969, a prestigious Committee on Reading was appointed by the National Academy of Education to examine America's reading problem and offer recommendations for improvement. Its report, "Toward a Literate Society," published in 1975, stated:

"It is not cynical to suggest that the chief beneficiaries of the Elementary and Secondary Education Act (ESEA) have been members of the school systems—both professional and paraprofessional—for whom new jobs were created... Seven years and as many billions of dollars later, the children of the poor have not been 'compensated' as clearly as the employees of the school systems through this investment."

A 1993 report, *Reinventing Chapter 1: The Current Chapter 1 Program and New Directions* (USDE, 1993), maintained that Title I programs reinforced low expectations of the students they served by providing remedial instruction and holding them to lower academic standards than other students. This report concluded that in order for the Title I program to effectively support all students in meeting challenging standards, fundamental change was required.

Increasingly, the core challenge to education became to be seen as family poverty. *Promising Results, Continuing Challenges: The Final Report of the National Assessment of Title I*, published by the US Department of Education Office of the Under Secretary Planning and Evaluation Service in 1999, stated this:

"Poverty is a significant problem for many of our nation's children. In 1997, the US Bureau of the Census estimated that 20 percent of American children under the age of 18 lived in poverty. This poverty rate is about the same level as in 1965 [the year in which Title I was first enacted], although it fluctuated during this period from a low of 15 percent in 1970 to a high of 22 percent in 1993. African American and Hispanic children—both with poverty rates of 37 percent—are more than twice as likely as non-Hispanic white children to be poor. Particularly in the urban core, communities are faced with concentrations of poverty that pose formidable challenges for schools. One-third of the children in America's cities live in poverty.

"Because the effects of poverty on learning are profound, these statistics translate into severe educational disadvantages for many children and pose serious challenges for public education. At the individual level, poverty has numerous correlates that inhibit learning. Poor children are more likely than wealthier children to be exposed to drug abuse, violence, and unhealthy living conditions. Low-income students are far more likely to drop out of school—in 1996, almost eight times more low-income students dropped out than high-income students did. Parents in economically disadvantaged families tend to have limited education and involvement in their children's learning. Teachers in schools with high concentrations of low-income students are less likely to have high expectations regarding their students' attainment of challenging academic standards, holding the students to lower standards than those for more advantaged students."

What this suggests is that pouring more money into schools is not an effective way of raising educational achievement if the students who walk through the doors every morning are hampered by the burdens of poverty.

The 1980 election of Ronald Reagan to the presidency sparked a significant reduction in federal education program funding as well as the beginning of a presidential effort to reduce the role of the federal government in domestic policy areas, namely public education. Throughout the 1980s, presidential and congressional support for ESEA fell sharply, with significantly fewer educationally disadvantaged children served under the law during this decade than in the 1970s.

The decision was made based on ideology to remove government from education at the federal level. Previous federal programs and bills were not assessed to determine their effectiveness.

For instance, the Education Consolidation and Improvement Act, passed in 1981 as part of President Reagan's Omnibus

Budget Reconciliation Act, reduced federal funding across most domestic policy areas. Under this act, Title I of ESEA was renamed Chapter 1. While Chapter 1 of ESEA retained its original legislative purpose of funding compensatory services for educationally disadvantaged students, significant reductions in federal aid and relaxed regulatory requirements led to fewer eligible students being served.

Thus while it may be argued that the Reagan doctrine of pulling back federal dollars from schools was somehow acceptable—because those dollars weren't doing much good anyway—his approach was for the federal government to do as little as possible in *any* area except military spending, and to toss important social and educational issues back into the laps of the states. Reagan sold Americans on his core vision: "Government is not the solution to our problem; government is the problem." Having charmed voters, Reagan convinced Americans that the government's only important roles were cutting taxes and funding the military.

Yet instead of bringing improvement to the bedrock drivers of educational success—robust employment, social stability, good neighborhoods—Reagan's approach accelerated a deindustrialization of the United States and a slump in the growth of American jobs, which declined 20 percent during the 1980s. The full Reaganomics "trickle-down" program brought not only tax cuts for the rich and corporations, it brought social spending cuts designed to offset the reduction in revenue created by the tax cuts. It also brought union busting, presumably to cut costs for business and create more capital that could then drive economic growth. But in order to have economic growth, consumers need to be able to spend on products other than sustenance and shelter.

Reducing wages of union workers pulled down the wages of nonunion workers as well, and shrunk the economy into which corporations wanted to sell their products. It was a serious error in economic policy whose effects still resonate even today.

A Nation at Risk

In 1983, the United States had yet another Sputnik moment: the publication of the report by President Ronald Reagan's National Commission on Excellence in Education. Entitled *A Nation at Risk: The Imperative for Educational Reform*, the report asserted that American schools were failing, igniting a new firestorm of local, state, and federal reform efforts.

The report surveyed various studies that pointed to academic underachievement on national and international scales. For example, the report noted that during the period from 1963 to 1980, average SAT scores dropped "over 50 points" in the verbal section and "nearly 40 points" in the mathematics section. Nearly 40 percent of seventeen-year-olds tested could not successfully "draw inferences from written material." Also, it revealed "only one-fifth can write a persuasive essay, and only one-third can solve a mathematics problem requiring several steps."

The report asserted that the United States was lagging behind other countries; according to tests conducted in the 1970s, on "nineteen academic tests American students were never first or second and, in comparison with other industrialized nations, were last seven times."

What did the report recommend?

The usual prescriptions: strengthened curriculums, higher standards, longer school days, better teachers. The report also noted that the federal government played an essential role in helping "meet the needs of key groups of students such as the gifted and talented, the socioeconomically disadvantaged, minority and language minority students, and the handicapped."

As for President Reagan, one of his campaign promises had been to shut down the US Department of Education, which had been—and still is—a favorite target of conservative politicians. Once elected, he never carried out his stated plan.

The report has been sharply criticized. As Salvatore Babones writes in his book *Sixteen for '16: A Progressive Agenda for a Better America*, the National Commission on Excellence in Education did little except recycle the same conclusions that politicians had been drawing for decades:

"It should come as no surprise that a commission dominated by administrators found that the problems of US schools were mainly caused by lazy students and unaccountable teachers. Administrative incompetence was not on the agenda. Nor were poverty, inequality, and racial discrimination. *A Nation at Risk* began from the assumption that our public schools were failing. Of course our public schools were failing. Our public schools are always failing. No investigative panel has ever found that our public schools are succeeding. But if public schools have been failing for so long—if they were already failing in 1983 and have been failing ever since—then very few of us alive today could possibly have had a decent education. So who are we to offer solutions for fixing these failing schools? We are ourselves the products of the very failing schools we propose to fix."

None of the report's recommendations addressed the underlying social and economic problems that had been keeping student achievement unacceptably low for decades.

It wasn't a problem of money. In the postwar era, money for public education had not been in short supply.

Over a forty-year period, in real dollars, average spending per student rose dramatically from $1,189 in 1950 to $5,237 in 1991.

From 1960 to 1991, the average salary of public school teachers rose 45 percent in real terms. Instructional staff in public schools generally saw their earnings increase faster than average full-time employees in other industries.

Student academic underachievement endured despite significant, ever increasing educational expenditures by federal, state, and local governments. During the 1990–91 school year, the United States spent more than $200 billion on public elementary and secondary education, which accounted for 3.8% of the 1991 United States gross domestic product (GDP). In comparison, during the same year Japan spent 2.8% of its GDP on elementary and secondary education. Indeed, one unifying theme in the history of modern American education was the consistent rise in inflation-adjusted spending.

Student performance did not keep pace with the dramatic increases in resources devoted to public education. Evidence from the National Assessment of Educational Progress and other performance measures revealed how poorly served America's public school students really were. Just 5 percent of seventeen-year-old high school students in 1988 could read well enough to understand and use information found in technical materials, literary essays, historical documents, and college-level texts. This percentage had been *falling* since 1971.

Between 1972 and 1991, average Scholastic Aptitude Test scores fell 41 points. This included scores for both black and white students. The number of students scoring over 600 on the verbal part of the SAT fell by 37 percent in the same period, so the overall decline couldn't be blamed on low-performing students dragging down the overall average.

In 1986, only 6 percent of eleventh graders could solve multistep math problems and use basic algebra. Seventy-five percent didn't know when Lincoln was president, and only one in five knew what Reconstruction was.

When compared to the scores of other industrialized nations, it was clear the United States consistently lagged behind. The United States spent more money per elementary and secondary school pupil than any other country, but without the expected results.

Between 1965 and 1992, more than ninety billion dollars was spent on Title I compensatory education funding for local education agencies and schools in areas with high rates of poverty. Despite this huge investment, there was scant evidence of any positive effect.

Pre- and post-tests administered to the same groups of students through a Department of Education study showed that little progress had been made among Title I students. Comparisons of similar groups of children by grade and poverty showed that program participation did not reduce the test score gap for disadvantaged students.

Studies showed that the benefits of additional class time spent in Title I instruction were too often undercut by missed class time. During 1991–1992, 70 percent of elementary classroom teachers reported that students missed some academic subject during Title I (which had been pointlessly renamed "Chapter 1" in 1981) reading/language arts instruction. Of this 70 percent, 56 percent indicated that students were missing regular reading/

language arts activities during their Title I reading/language arts instruction.

Many would argue that the design of the program had flaws. How can we expect students who are already behind to be pulled out of their reading and math classes to remediate identified skills while still being responsible for the lessons in the regular classroom?

Another significant problem with Title I was an incentive structure that discouraged reaching the very end for which the program was created. Since funds were allocated based on the number of educationally disadvantaged children in a district, as test scores rose, so did the risk of losing program money. Therefore the system had a built-in incentive to perpetuate itself by finding more disadvantaged children and keeping them in the program.

Ironically, having a large population of educationally disadvantaged children ensured continued funding. As we have seen too many times before, the doctor prescribes the expensive placebo and everyone goes home, satisfied that action has been taken to cure the patient. The taxpayer foots the bill for the placebo—and then wonders why the world always seems the same and the patient never feels any better.

Improving America's
Schools Act—1994

During the 1988 US presidential campaign, candidate George H. W. Bush, who was the sitting vice president, told a group of students: "I want to be the education president. I want to lead a renaissance of quality in our schools."

Unlike his old boss Ronald Reagan, George Bush didn't talk about abolishing the Department of Education. With the memory of *A Nation at Risk* still fresh in the minds of voters, the solutions to the perceived problems of America's public schools remained the familiar standbys: improve the curriculum, get better teachers, spend more federal money.

Having gotten himself elected to the nation's highest office, in late September 1989 President Bush called the nation's governors to a two-day summit in Charlottesville, Virginia, to discuss a single policy issue: education. The gathering—which included a future president, Arkansas Governor Bill Clinton—was to be a crucial point in the push for standards-based education accountability.

The subsequent reviews of the summit suggested that it was all talk and no action. Suzanne Fields of *The Los Angeles Times Syndicate* wrote:

"Whatever President Bush's education summit with the governors launched, it wasn't a Sputnik. The satellite the Soviets propelled into orbit in 1957 gave American educators the shot of adrenaline that propelled their students into the Space Age. Math and science suddenly got top priority.

"But that was then and this is now.

"In international competitions today, American students finish last in math and science and go to the head of the class in couch-potato studies... The education summiteers, aware of the problems, got high on consensus without their imaginations having to leave the ground."

The next year, halfway through Bush's term, most education observers believed the self-proclaimed education leader was not meeting expectations.

The president's first secretary of education, Lauro F. Cavazos, was widely viewed as an ineffective advocate for education reform whom Bush should have fired. A presidential package of education initiatives went down to defeat in the last days of the 101st Congress, and a legislative proposal related to his call for "partial deregulation" of the nation's schools died with it. The Bush administration's plans to introduce its own initiative to free schools from regulation never got off the ground.

The Bush administration even became embroiled in a civil rights debacle when Assistant Secretary of Education Michael L. Williams declared that many scholarships awarded on the basis of race violated federal law.

In 1992, Bill Clinton, a popular Democratic governor of Arkansas who had been instrumental in the 1989 Charlottesville education summit and the formulation of the national education goals, defeated Bush and was elected president. Clinton's campaign against President Bush had focused strongly on commitment to federal action for education. He had drawn on ideas promoted at the Charlottesville summit and the work of the National Education Goals Panel, on which he served. In addition, he carried forth initiatives from the previous Congress and built on the work of the states undertaking reform. For his secretary of education, Clinton chose Richard Riley, a popular former governor of South Carolina who had been active with the Southern Regional Education Board in its work to raise standards and performance in the South. Riley would serve with Clinton all eight years he was in office, making him the longest-tenured secretary of education in history.

Clinton's first legislative proposal—and success—was called Goals 2000: The Educate America Act, which we'll discuss in the following chapter.

At the same time, the president developed and advocated for the renewal of ESEA, but with substantial changes; the renewed act would be renamed Improving America's Schools Act, or IASA. Clinton wanted Goals 2000 enacted first, so it would set state standards and tests for the reauthorized act; he did not want Goals 2000 and IASA to be commingled, fearing that any additional money that might be garnered for Goals 2000 would simply be siphoned off to support Title I and not the broader systemic reforms he envisioned. Goals 2000 was signed into law in March 1994, and then in October the president signed IASA into law.

IASA provided the authority for a $10 billion appropriation in aid to states and localities. The new federal legislation moved away from setting program-specific requirements and toward promoting the use of federal funds to support locally designed approaches to improving the quality of teaching and learning in schools. The goal was to bring all the pieces together in a systemic way to upgrade schools. IASA coordinated federal resources and policies with preexisting efforts at the state and local levels to improve instruction.

In a statement released in September 1995, Secretary of Education Richard Wiley provided a summary of the administration's view of the most important features of IASA.

The statement asserted that the Education Department's research supported the following four key elements of a comprehensive education improvement effort:

1. **High standards for all students.**
   In an increasingly complex and diverse society and an economic environment that will be dominated by high-skilled jobs, today's students must meet high academic standards in order to succeed. Research and practice suggest that all students can learn to meet far more challenging academic standards than we currently expect of them. The IASA provides resources to states, districts, and schools to support their efforts to help students reach high state standards.

2. **Teachers better trained for teaching to high standards.**
   Professional development for teachers, principals, and other school staff is critical to creating and sustaining the learning environments necessary to help all students reach higher levels of achievement.
   The new Title I emphasizes high quality teaching and professional development. State, district, and school

plans will outline strategies for providing teachers,
administrators, other school staff, and district-level
personnel with the kind of professional development
they need to help ensure that low-achieving students in
high-poverty schools meet challenging standard.

3. **Flexibility to stimulate local reform, coupled with accountability for results.**
   The IASA revises the ESEA to provide broad
   flexibility to states, school districts, and schools in their
   implementation of federal programs. At the same time,
   the IASA calls for strategies to hold school districts and
   schools accountable for improved student achievement.

4. **Close partnerships among families, communities, and schools.**
   Research and practice show that substantial, ongoing
   family involvement in children's learning is a critical
   link to achieving a high-quality education and a safe,
   disciplined learning environment.

The measures put forth in the act, and the strengthening
of Title I, the major funnel of federal dollars to public schools,
certainly sounded like a bold initiative. Perhaps the nation could
be no longer at risk.

And yet, despite the renewed effort and the flow of federal
funds into schools, the problems stubbornly persisted. The doctor
had again prescribed the tasty sugar pill, the patient was sent
home, and everyone congratulated each other because decisive
action had been taken.

The US Education Statistics Report

In April 1998, the US Department of Education published a report entitled *Achievement in the United States: Progress Since "A Nation at Risk"?* Authored by Pascal D. Forgione Jr., PhD, the US commissioner of education statistics, while the report offered a few bright spots, the overall picture was unimpressive.

The bright spots included a decline in the high school dropout rate, an increase in the educational aspirations and college attendance rates of high school seniors, and increases in the academic course load of high school students.

The rest was a mixed bag. In math and science, "Long-term trends in science and mathematics show declines in the 1970s and early 1980s, followed by modest increases. For example, the mathematics score averages of seventeen-year-olds declined from 1973 to 1982, then increased to a level in 1996 similar to the 1973 level."

Long-term trends in reading achievement showed some improvement across the assessment years for elementary students, but not high schoolers. As the report stated, "In 1996, the average reading score for nine-year-olds was higher than it was in 1971. Thirteen-year-olds showed moderate gains in reading achievement; in 1996, their average reading score was higher than that in 1971. There was an overall pattern of increase in reading scores for seventeen-year-olds, but the 1996 average score was not significantly different than in 1971."

The mathematics and science achievement gap between white, black, and Hispanic students had narrowed somewhat since *A Nation at Risk.* Blacks and Hispanics in each of the age groups tested (nine-, thirteen-, and seventeen-year-olds) tended to make larger gains than whites during this period. But, "paradoxically, the achievement gains of each of these major subgroups are larger than that for the nation as a whole because of compositional changes in the student population. In particular, the lowest scoring subgroups represent a greater share of the population in 1996 than in earlier years."

How the US compared with other countries was discouraging. Data from the Third International Mathematics and Science Study (TIMSS) suggested that the relative international standing of US students declined as they progressed through school. "In both subject areas [of math and science]," said the report, "our students perform above the international average in grade four, close to the international average in grade eight, and considerably below it in grade twelve... In twelfth grade, the achievement scores of both our overall student population tested on general mathematics and science knowledge, and of our more advanced students tested in mathematics and physics, were well below the international average."

Perhaps most significantly, the report suggested what many educators had long suspected. "Findings from TIMSS," said the report, "suggest that many of the 'cure-alls' recommended in the past are not associated with high performance in all nations. While strategies such as more homework, more seat time, and less television may be important in improving the achievement of individual students and schools, they do not appear to be potent variables in explaining cross-national student achievement differences." There is no "one-size-fits-all" solution to better education, and no magic pill that the education doctor can prescribe to every school. We need to do what works—and no solution works in every situation.

IASA's school improvement measures proved disappointing to many reformers. IASA required states and school districts to identify schools in need of school improvement. Schools that continued to perform poorly would be identified for a more aggressive intervention. By 2001, it was increasingly clear that many schools were languishing on federal school improvement and corrective action lists with little change. In fact, many schools did not even know they were on the lists; or if they were on the lists, they didn't know why.

While the intent of the IASA was to create single and "seamless" accountability systems that would treat all schools equally, by 2000–2001 only twenty-two states had single accountability systems in place. Of course, there is no one type of school; every school has its own individual characteristics. A one-size-fits-all solution is not going to work.

More than half of the states had parallel accountability systems, in which Title I schools were subject to a different measure of adequate yearly progress (AYP). States also varied in the percentage of students that schools were expected to bring up to their "proficient" standard, timelines for meeting these performance goals, and the degree to which their Title I AYP definitions included standards of continuous progress. There was no federal requirement to close the gap, and only one-third of the states focused on closing the gap between low- and high-achieving students in their Title I schools. Few states required schools to close achievement gaps between economically disadvantaged and economically advantaged students, between English-dominant and limited English-speaking students, between white students and students of color, or between students with and without disabilities.

The growing mountains of evidence confirmed that pouring more money into schools—the "*do something*" approach—did not attack the root problems of poor student achievement and had minimal positive effect relative to the vast sums being spent.

Goals 2000:
Educate America Act

On March 31, 1994, President Bill Clinton signed into law the Goals 2000: Educate America Act. The stated purpose of the act was to provide resources to states and communities to ensure that all students reached their full potential.

It was based on the premise of outcomes-based education, which says that students will reach higher levels of achievement when more is expected of them.

With the act came the lingering memory of *A Nation at Risk*. Secretary of Education Richard Riley said at the inaugural meeting for Goals 2000, "Some of you will use the new provisions of Goals 2000 to expand what you have started. Some of you will use it to reinvigorate and connect existing reforms. And others of you may use it to launch a comprehensive new effort to improve teaching and learning. That's really what we're about isn't it? But how you use Goals 2000 to encourage learning back home is really your choice. I urge you to think big, to think comprehensively, to recognize that this won't happen in a year or in just a few years. We spent ten years getting to the point where we had the support to pass Goals 2000. *A Nation at Risk* was ten years ago. We will probably spend another ten years making it work for all of our children."

Three times in the previous six years, Congress had attempted to pass education reform legislation, and each time it had been unable to resolve its differences. The strong bipartisan support for Goals 2000 seemed to show that the nation was ready to move from "a nation at risk" to a nation moving forward.

The enactment of Goals 2000 was touted as the beginning of a new era in school and education reform—a revolutionary, all-inclusive plan to change every aspect of the nation's education system, while at the same time aligning its individual parts with one another.

The eight primary goals stated in the Summary of Goals 2000 included:

By the Year 2000...
1. All children in America will start school ready to learn.
2. The high school graduation rate will increase to at least 90 percent.
3. All students will leave grades 4, 8, and 12 having demonstrated competency over challenging subject matter including English, mathematics, science, foreign languages, civics and government, economics, the arts, history, and geography, and every school in America will ensure that all students learn to use their minds well, so they may be prepared for responsible citizenship, further learning, and productive employment in our nation's modern economy.
4. United States students will be first in the world in mathematics and science achievement.

5. Every adult American will be literate and will possess the knowledge and skills necessary to compete in a global economy and exercise the rights and responsibilities of citizenship.
6. Every school in the United States will be free of drugs, violence, and the unauthorized presence of firearms and alcohol and will offer a disciplined environment conducive to learning.
7. The nation's teaching force will have access to programs for the continued improvement of their professional skills and the opportunity to acquire the knowledge and skills needed to instruct and prepare all American students for the next century.
8. Every school will promote partnerships that will increase parental involvement and participation in promoting the social, emotional, and academic growth of children.

These were lofty goals indeed.

Goal number one—"All children in America will start school ready to learn"—seemed to address the underlying economic issues that had historically driven poor student performance in school. As commentary by the University of Notre Dame pointed out, "Goal 1 is needed because almost half of American babies start life behind and never have the support to catch up. Forty-five percent of our children are born with risk factors for further learning and development deficiencies. Only thirty-seven percent are immunized by age two against major childhood diseases. Just over half of our preschool children are read to daily (53%), and only forty-three percent are involved in discussions about family history or ethnic heritage."

For fiscal year 1994, in support of Goals 2000 Congress appropriated $105 million. The federal government took pains to reassure the states that the act was not a federal takeover of schools. Section 318 stated, "Nothing in this Act shall be construed to authorize an officer or employee of the Federal Government to mandate, direct, or control a State, local educational agency, or school's curriculum, program of instruction, or allocation of State or local resources or mandate a State or any subdivision thereof to spend any funds or incur any costs not paid for under this Act." The main goal of the Goals 2000 Act were to encourage local school systems into meeting educational needs, help students reach their potential, increase parental involvement, and improve teachers' skills.

And oh, yes, Sputnik got mentioned. In *The Daily Report Card* of Monday, June 12, 1995, educators and policy makers were asked how Goals 2000 was helping them reform education. LeGrande Baldwin, the lead principal, Cluster 4, Maury School, Washington, DC, replied as follows:

"Goals 2000 is as significant as the launching of Sputnik. It is an initiative that redirects our focus in terms of improving the quality of education and life in this country. These goals provide our blueprint for meeting the challenges of the twenty-first century."

The Inevitable Intrusion of Politics

Almost immediately, some of the key components of Goals 2000 became caught up in political conflict.

As Kerry diGrazia wrote in the *Baltimore Sun* on April 9, 1995, "The high-minded ideals of Goals 2000 seem universal.

Who could dispute the importance of sending children to school 'ready to learn' or the need for schools 'free of drugs and violence'—two of the eight National Education Goals? But support for Goals 2000 erodes with the looming prospect of national curriculum standards—standards designed to provide a way to meet the goal that 'all students will leave grades 4, 8 and 12 having demonstrated competency over challenging subject matter.'"

In the autumn of 1994, suggestions for "challenging subject matter" had been released by various education experts and agencies for math, arts, geography, history, and civics. Standards in science, economics, foreign languages, English, and reading were in various stages of development.

Development of such standards had been initially supported by the administration of George H. W. Bush, which provided federal funds for the development panels, and then embraced by the Clinton administration.

But the November 1994 Republican sweep of congressional elections had turned what had seemed like a consensus into a heated debate both within the education community and among politicians in Washington. The "Republican Revolution" was the first time in forty years that the Republicans had a majority in both houses of Congress. Speaker Newt Gingrich's "Contract with America" was a ten-point program that the new Republican majority said it would enact in its first one hundred days in office. The contract's planks had titles like the Fiscal Responsibility Act, the Taking Back Our Streets Act, and the Personal Responsibility Act. Its purpose, plain and simple, was to shrink the federal social safety net—the thirteen categories of federal welfare programs that provide benefits to individuals or families, including Social Security, Medicare, and Unemployment.

Goals 2000 became a target. The history standards, in particular, were criticized for going too far to satisfy "political correctness." Lynne V. Cheney, the wife of future Vice President Dick Cheney, and who had chaired the National Endowment for the Humanities during the Reagan and Bush administrations, complained, "The things that we have done that are successes, the triumphs, the progress that we have made have not been given sufficient emphasis, so that students learning history would have a very warped view of our past."

In an opinion column published in *The Evening Sun*, she wrote, "The American history standards make it seem that Joseph McCarthy and McCarthyism—mentioned nineteen times—are far more important than George Washington—mentioned twice—or Thomas Edison—mentioned not at all."

In January, in a vote of ninety-nine to one, the US Senate condemned the history standards. Incoming Republican committee chairmen in both houses vowed to pass bills to kill the National Education Standards and Improvement Council, a board that was to review state and national standards and to which no members have yet been named. It was anticipated that the job of reviewing standards would probably be taken over by the National Education Goals Panel, whose members were primarily state officials.

Bruce Manno, a senior fellow at the Washington-based Hudson Institute, said that many of the outcomes targeted by Goals 2000 could be difficult to measure because they concerned attitudes and values rather than academic achievement. Conservatives were afraid that national curriculum standards would take control of education from families and political leaders and give it to Education Department specialists.

The US Department of Education tried to deflect criticism of national curriculum standards, and in all of the Goals 2000 literature the key word became "voluntary." Department of Education reports and officials were careful to emphasize that curriculum standards are models and should supplement, rather than supplant, state and community efforts to improve education.

The new Congress targeted federal welfare and other social programs, with more than one hundred federal programs to be abolished and replaced with grants to states, where lawmakers at the state levels could reduce benefits and spending even further. To reduce the welfare rolls, Speaker Gingrich even proposed opening orphanages, and sought to bar legal immigrants from federal programs such as student loans, school lunches, and disability payments for the elderly.

In June 1995, Republicans crafted a supplemental appropriations/recissions bill (HR 1158). The GOP majority set a political trap for President Clinton: While a portion of the bill provided financial assistance to earthquake-damaged California and other flood-stricken states, House leaders used the recissions portion of the bill to defund some of Clinton's domestic programs and legislative accomplishments made during his first two years in office, including Americorps and Goals 2000. The bill passed the House. In the Senate version of the bill, the president successfully won back $835 million in rescinded funds, but House-Senate conferees ignored the compromise and pushed forth with a $16.4 billion package of cuts that the administration had rejected.

A veto of the bill, which also contained aid for Oklahoma City subsequent to the bombing of the Murrah Federal Building, was risky for Clinton, but veto it he did.

In April 1997, conservative activist Phyllis Schlafly provided the opposition view in *The Phyllis Schlafly Report* when she wrote, "Local control is out. President Clinton made a speech on January 22 to a group identified by the White House as 'the students, parents and teachers of the Northbrook Area Schools Consortium.' One line in his speech was greeted by stony silence. That's when he said, 'We can no longer hide behind our love of local control of the schools.'

"That was a telltale admission that the real goal of the Clinton Administration's education plan is to eliminate local control of public schools.

"Goals 2000 is part of a coordinated national plan to impose federal mandates, bypass local control, and eliminate accountability. Once a state accepts Goals 2000 funding, it must implement Goals 2000's national goals and objectives. Section 318 pretends to prohibit federal control of curriculum, but that's just a placebo, because the statute includes dozens of specific mandates about curriculum, instructional materials, standards, content, and assessments."

As much as they opposed a federal takeover of local schools, here's what conservatives really hated, as Schlafly wrote: "The Goals 2000 statute codifies the eight national education goals. But the goals themselves are defective, particularly the first goal, 'By the year 2000, all children in America will start school ready to learn.' Many schools are using this language to bring health clinics and a wide array of social services into the public schools, financed in devious ways through Medicaid. This is one cause of the tremendous increase in Medicaid costs, and it's part of the Administration's plan to bring the rejected Clinton proposal for socialized medicine in through the schoolhouse door."

As the political battles raged, performance among underprivileged students persistently lagged. As David Osher, vice president and institute fellow at American Institutes for Research, wrote in October 2013 about *A Nation at Risk*, which had been published thirty years earlier, "Academic progress, nation building, and equity may lag today partly because of how the report conceptualized risk and partly because of how that risk was interpreted. The National Commission on Excellence in Education, which wrote the report... stopped short of addressing how poverty and discrimination affects learning and how opportunities to learn are allocated. Nor did they identify ways to fund adequate education for all in light of the Supreme Court's 1973 *San Antonio Independent School District v. Rodriguez* decision, which legitimated school funding based on property taxes.

"As another example of good intentions never translated into hard-hitting recommendations, the commission members also said they didn't 'believe that a public commitment to excellence and educational reform must be made at the expense of a strong public commitment to the equitable treatment of our diverse population' and articulated the 'twin goals of equity and high-quality schooling.' But the commissioners' recommendations didn't address the many factors that affect attendance, engagement, learning, and test performance—so-called conditions for learning. Focusing narrowly on the students' 'hard work, self-discipline, and motivation' without attention to these other enabling factors blunted the force of the important call for higher standards and achievement."

Goals 2000 was further crippled by the federal government's tepid enforcement of its own stated performance standards for schools. The 1994 reauthorization of the Elementary and Secondary Education Act required states to develop content and performance standards for K–12 schools. Congress also adopted the concept of "adequate yearly progress" (AYP) that later became the centerpiece of accountability in the No Child Left Behind Act of 2001. States were required to demonstrate "continuous and substantial" progress toward the goal of academic proficiency for all students. However, there was no stated deadline, and consequences for failure were largely absent from the law. States were supposed to have standards in place by 1997–98, and assessments and final definitions of adequate yearly progress by 2000–01. But as Andrew Rudalevige wrote in "The Politics of No Child Left Behind" in *EducationNext*, the Clinton administration never withheld funds from states that failed to meet these timelines. The White House, concerned that flexing federal muscle would provoke the Republican Congress, focused on providing states with assistance in the development process. As of the original 1997 deadline, the American Federation of Teachers found that just seventeen states had "clear and specific standards" in English, math, social studies, and science.

The lesson that many analysts and policymakers took from the 1994 reauthorization was that the flow of federal money needed to be more closely aligned with measurable gains in student performance. Rudalevige wrote that in April 1999, Andrew Rotherham of the Democratic Leadership Council's Progressive Policy Institute summed up the key elements of this view by saying that Congress, to rectify the Title I program's status as "an undertaking without consequences" for everyone except students, should set performance benchmarks and terminate aid to districts that failed to meet them.

As usual, the federal doctor had prescribed a sugar pill, and politicians patted themselves on the back for having taken action to cure the patient. Meanwhile, our schools remained sick.

No Child Left Behind

In the winter of 1999, Texas governor George W. Bush was running for president and pitching himself as a "compassionate conservative."

As far as education was concerned, the "compassion" was for students held back by what Bush called "the soft bigotry of low expectations." In other words, underperforming students were victims not of economic and social oppression but of low expectations. The theory was that if we demanded better results from underprivileged young people, by magic they'd step up and deliver.

The "conservative" part of the equation lay in the familiar prescription of getting the federal government out of the business of the states, fostering parental choice, and returning to local spending authority. On education policy Bush was closer to the center than many in his own party, and when the 2000 Republican platform was being written he opposed language calling for the abolition of the Department of Education—a favorite goal for conservatives even today.

Education reform had been a major issue in Texas, and, like his father before him, Bush realized its potential as a Republican

63

presidential position. As governor, Bush had backed the state's programs of annually testing students in grades three through eight and rating schools based on their performance on the Texas Assessment of Academic Skills (TAAS) exam. On the campaign trail he pointed to steadily improving TAAS scores, particularly among black and Latino students.

Soon after Bush's victory was confirmed, the president-elect invited about twenty members of Congress to Austin, Texas, to discuss what to do about the problems in American education. A piece of draft legislation was already available in the form of Bush's campaign position paper on the topic, "No Child Left Behind." The title had been cribbed from "Leave No Child Behind," the left-leaning Children's Defense Fund's trademarked mission statement.

When Congress convened in January 2001, No Child Left Behind (NCLB) quickly emerged as a thirty-page legislative blueprint. After making its way through Congress with bipartisan support—including from Senator Edward Kennedy—President Bush signed it into law on January 8, 2002. Politicians and some educators applauded the government's willingness to act quickly to *do something* to fix American education.

To the satisfaction of conservative politicians, the menu of things that needed to be done fell largely not on the back of the federal government but on the backs of the states and local school districts. Central to No Child Left Behind was a set of interconnected requirements in various functional areas that each state needed to fulfill:

Standards and Testing
- Each state was required to develop and implement its own "challenging" academic standards in reading and math.
- Annual statewide progress objectives were to be set to ensure that all groups of students reached proficiency within twelve years (that is, by 2014).
- To measure student progress in reading and math, children would be tested annually in grades three through eight.

Accountability
- The test results of each school would be published in an annual "report card" detailing how that school was performing. The statewide results would be aggregated into a consolidated report for each state showing how the state was progressing overall toward its proficiency objectives. To help ensure that all groups of students were progressing at an adequate rate, the test results would be broken out and reported according to poverty, race, ethnicity, disability, and limited English proficiency. This was known as "disaggregation of data" and was intended to prevent schools from grouping test results together into one overall average for the school, which would effectively hide the achievement gaps between groups of students.

Adequate Yearly Progress
- States would have until the 2005–06 school year to develop and implement their tests. Once in place, schools and districts would be required to demonstrate

"adequate yearly progress" (AYP) toward their statewide objectives. The goal was to show, through their test scores, that they were on course to reach proficiency for all groups of students within twelve years.

States would receive federal funds to help develop their tests. A "trigger mechanism" specified that states were *not* required to develop the reading and math tests for grades three through eight if the federal government failed to provide the necessary funding. (This was just one of the many loopholes in NCLB that allowed the states to sidestep many of the law's requirements.)

If a school's results were repeatedly substandard, then measures would be taken to improve the school. The measures increased in severity with each passing year of poor performance, according to the following scale:

Year two of missing AYP: The offending school would be publicly labeled as in need of improvement, which would presumably both shame it and raise the threat that parents of means would pull their children out, leaving even more disadvantaged kids behind. The second-year school was also required to develop a two-year improvement plan for the subject(s) in which the school was deficient.

Year three: The school had to offer free tutoring and other supplemental education services to low-performing students. It was unclear who would pay for these additional services.

Year four: The school was branded as requiring "corrective action," which could involve introduction of a new curriculum, wholesale replacement of staff, or extending the amount of time students spent in class. Again, how these measures would be funded was unclear.

Year five: Restructuring the entire school. The plan would be implemented if the school failed to hit its AYP targets for the sixth year in a row. Options included closing the school, turning the school into a charter school, hiring a private company to run the school (presumably this would be Vice President Dick Cheney's favorite option), or asking the state office of education to run the school directly.

Each year, the state and school report cards would be released showing the performance of students disaggregated by ethnic and economic subgroups. As verification of the results from state assessments, states would be required to participate in the National Assessment of Educational Progress (NAEP) each year, and schools receiving Title I compensatory-education funds would be required to show that disadvantaged students were making adequate yearly progress.

Those schools that fell behind would be subject to various "school improvement," "corrective action," or "restructuring" measures imposed by the state. Underperforming schools could avoid such measures if they could demonstrate a 10 percent reduction in the number of students that were not meeting the annual proficiency goals.

The NAEP Benchmark

To placate politicians and educators who were opposed to any federal interference in school curriculums, NCLB specifically prohibited any "national testing" or "federally controlled curriculum." It was left up to each state to select and/or design its own tests, and to make sure that the tests were aligned with that state's curriculum standards.

While the idea of federal standards in education was political poison, the problem was approached obliquely through the National Assessment of Educational Progress (NAEP). An independent project mandated by the US Congress, today, as it did then, NAEP goes into the classroom to develop and provide data on student achievement in various subjects, which is then released as *The Nation's Report Card*. There are no results for individual students, classrooms, or schools. NAEP reports results for different demographic groups, including gender, socioeconomic status, and race/ethnicity. Assessments are given most frequently in mathematics, reading, science, and writing. Other subjects such as the arts, civics, economics, geography, and US history are assessed periodically.

In addition to assessing student achievement in various subjects, NAEP also collects information from students, teachers, and schools to help provide contextual information about the assessments and factors that may be related to students' learning.

An NAEP test would be given to a small sample of each state's fourth and eighth-grade students in reading and math every other year. This provision, known as "NAEP comparability," was supposed to ensure that states were not setting their educational standards too low. For example, if a state claimed progress on its statewide test results but did not show comparable progress on the NAEP, the discrepancy would suggest that the state's standards and tests were not challenging enough. No Child Left Behind, however, did not provide for any penalties if a state's test scores fell behind relative to its NAEP results; it only required that the comparative results be made public.

The Murky Role of the Federal Government

Politically, NCLB seemed like a bold initiative from a new president who was determined to make a difference.

In reality, it was a slippery piece of business. As one commentator wrote, the complex program was "at once numbingly detailed and comfortably vague."

Amid all the back-and-forth, one reality was often overlooked. As Alexander "Sandy" Kress, senior advisor to President George W. Bush on education with respect to the No Child Left Behind Act of 2001, put it, the federal government is just a "seven percent investor in a huge company owned by someone else." The other 93 percent of K–12 public education funding comes from states and localities. This limits the degree of change the federal government can leverage. Even if it were willing to use a stick, the one carried by the Department of Education was relatively small. The law's commitment to the success of every child made it hard to compromise on the adequate yearly progress requirements, but this did not make it feasible policy.

The passage of legislation was only the beginning of the story. The political compromises written into NCLB gave the states and schools plenty of wriggle room. Draft rules on testing released in March 2002 indicated that states would be allowed to use different tests in different areas, potentially undercutting their comparability. The Department of Education also distanced itself from judging the quality of state standards and assessments. The rules released in July 2002 allowed states to use either criterion-referenced tests linked to state standards or norm-referenced tests that measured how students performed compared with their peers, modified somewhat to reflect state standards. It was unclear whether states would be forced to develop standards-driven tests or whether "augmented" commercial exams would be ultimately acceptable.

This flexibility suited both the states and Washington politicians. In July 2002, for example, the Department of Education listed some 8,600 schools that had failed to meet state standards for two consecutive years. In response, some states began to quietly lower their standards. In an October letter to state school chiefs, Department of Education head Roderick Paige warned that state plans to "ratchet down their standards in order to remove schools from their lists of low performers" were "nothing less than shameful."

It's unclear whether any school was ever shut down solely because of failure to meet NCLB standards. A March 2013 report by the Pennsylvania Clearinghouse for Education Research (PACER) stated, "The nation's largest school districts have increasingly turned to building closures to address budget deficits, demographic shifts, and the movement of students to charter schools. Over the past decade, seventy large or mid-sized cities have closed schools—averaging eleven buildings per closure." While the influence of NCLB may be a factor, state education budgets—far more central to school funding than federal investments—tightened after the onset of the Great Recession. In the 2012–13 school year, twenty-six states spent less per pupil than the previous year. After adjusting for inflation, thirty-five states are now spending less than before the recession. At the local level, many districts—especially in urban areas—are experiencing persistent declines in enrollment as a result of population shifts and increasing charter school attendance.

Under No Child Left Behind, students in underperforming schools were to be offered the chance to attend a better-performing school in their district. But other schools were under *no legal obligation* to accept the transferring student. The promise by NCLB that your child could get a transfer to a better school was largely hollow.

In this case, the education doctor had promised to provide treatment that was simply not available.

The Federal Cash Machine

At the end of the day, it's all about the money—or, at least, *promising* money.

To show their support for NCLB, the Bush administration and Congress backed huge increases in funding for elementary and secondary education. Funds came in the form of programs that distributed money directly to local schools for their use, as well as grant programs, where particular schools or groups applied directly to the federal government for funding.

From 2001, the fiscal year before the law's passage, to fiscal year 2004, total federal education funding increased from $42.2 billion to $55.7 billion. A billion federal dollars was earmarked for a new Reading First program, and over $100 million for its companion, Early Reading First.

In total, according to the US Department of Education, federal funding for education increased 59.8% from 2000 to 2003.

The NCLB increases paralleled another significant increase in federal education funding at that time for the Individuals with Disabilities Education Act (IDEA). IDEA Part B, a state formula-funding program that distributed money to local districts for the education of students with disabilities, was increased from $6.3 billion in 2001 to $10.1 billion in 2004. Because a district's and state's performance on NCLB measures depended on improved performance by students with learning disabilities, this 60 percent increase in funding was also an important part of the overall approach to NCLB implementation.

As usual, federal cash came with expensive strings attached.

Several provisions of NCLB, such as a push for quality teachers and more professional development, placed additional demands on local districts and state education agencies that were not fully reimbursed by increased levels of federal NCLB funding.

Not a few commentators asserted that the level of funding was not enough. Senator Ted Kennedy, one of the initial sponsors of NCLB, said, "The tragedy is that these long overdue reforms are finally in place, but the funds are not."

Susan B. Neuman, the Department of Education's former assistant secretary for elementary and secondary education, said, "In [the most disadvantaged schools] in America, even the most earnest teacher has often given up because they lack every available resource that could possibly make a difference... When we say all children can achieve and then not give them the additional resources... we are creating a fantasy."

Then there's the gap between what Washington *says* it's going to pay for and what it *actually* pays for. Any act can be passed and signed into law but not fully funded. It's all part of Washington's persistent impulse to *do something* without fully exploring the problem and figuring out what it will take over many years to fix it. Appropriations bills always originate in the House of Representatives, and neither the Senate nor the White House ever requested federal funding up to the authorized levels for several of the main provisions of NCLB. In 2006, for example, President Bush requested only $13.3 billion of a possible $22.75 billion in funding for NCLB. President Bush's 2008 budget proposal allotted $61 billion for the Education Department—a *decrease* of $1.3 billion from the year before. Funding for the Enhancing Education Through Technology Program (EETT) continued to drop while the demand for technology in schools increased.

By way of explanation, members of Congress often characterize authorized spending levels as spending *targets*, not spending *guarantees*. More than one opponent has argued that funding shortfalls meant that schools faced with mandated penalties for failing to meet testing targets were denied the resources necessary to fix the problems revealed by testing. In fiscal year 2007, $75 billion in costs were shifted from NCLB, adding further stresses on state budgets. This decrease meant that schools were forced to cut programs that served to educate children, which then impaired the schools' ability to meet the goals of NCLB.

The net result was that either decreases in funding or flat funding came at a time when there was an increase in expectations for school performance. To make up the shortfall and to achieve the national educational goals set by NCLB, many schools were forced to reallocate funds that had been intended for other purposes, such as sports and art. For example, in 2007 National Public Radio cited a report by the Center on Education Policy that revealed "the complex formula used to calculate how much each district gets has led to wild swings in funding, so California is contending with a five percent drop in Title I funding. In Florida, the total drop is more like nine percent. Some urban districts, including high-poverty areas like New York City, Houston and Atlanta, are taking the heaviest cuts."

The number one area where funding was cut from the national budget was in Title I funding for disadvantaged students and schools.

Standardized Testing and Teaching to the Test

Traditionally, states have enjoyed great freedom in setting their own standards for public education. This approach may have made sense in the eighteenth century, when the Union was a loose confederation of states and it took five days to travel from Philadelphia to Boston on horseback. While the idea that American students in the twenty-first century should share a common curriculum and standards for achievement may seem like a no-brainer to progressive educators, critics of NCLB have argued that the focus only on standardized *testing*—without a corresponding agreement about a standardized *curriculum*—has had a toxic side effect: it encourages teachers to teach a narrow subset of skills that the school believes increases test performance, therefore keeping the flow of federal dollars coming and the annoying Department of Education off their backs.

Evidence suggests that incentives for adequate yearly improvement (AYP) and teaching to the test caused some states to lower their educational standards. Because each state can produce its own standardized tests, to increase student scores a state can make its statewide tests easier. The *Washington Post* reported that Missouri, for example, improved test scores but openly admitted that they lowered the standards. Gene Wilhoit, executive director of the Council of Chief State School Officers, said it was understandable that some states would set lower standards. "They're trying to make sense out of this. They're trying to survive."

According to the *Washington Post*, a study by the Washington-based children's advocacy group Ed Trust showed that in Mississippi, of those fourth graders who took state reading tests, 89 percent were deemed proficient or better in reading. But on the National Assessment of Educational Progress, a federal standard, only 18 percent were deemed proficient.

In Oklahoma, 75 percent of fourth graders were proficient or better in math on the state test, while on the federal test, only 29 percent met that standard.

In Massachusetts, 50 percent of fourth graders were proficient in reading on state tests, compared with 44 percent on the national test.

A 2007 study by the US Department of Education indicated that the observed differences in states' reported scores was largely due to differences in the stringency of their standards.

Dropout rates were another metric that schools could manipulate. To reduce unfavorable statistics, schools were shown to employ "creative reclassification" of high school dropouts. For example, as Deborah Meier and George Wood cited in their book *Many Children Left Behind: How the No Child Left Behind Act Is Damaging Our Children and Our Schools*, at Sharpstown High School in Houston, Texas, more than one thousand students began high school as freshmen. Four years later, fewer than three hundred were enrolled in the senior class. In 2001, for example, four hundred and sixty-three students left school. However, *none* of these missing students from Sharpstown High were reported as dropouts—the reason for leaving was changed to "transferred to another school or district." After demonstrating a "successful" reduction in the school's dropout rate, the school was awarded with a National Award for Excellence.

"That's how you get to zero dropouts," said Robert Kimball, an assistant principal at Sharpstown High School, to reporter Rebecca Leung from *60 Minutes*. "By assigning codes that say, 'Well, this student, you know, went to another school. He did this or that.' And basically, all four hundred and sixty-three students disappeared. And the school reported zero dropouts for the year. They were not counted as dropouts, so the school had an outstanding record."

Sharpstown High wasn't the only "outstanding" school. The Houston school district reported an amazingly low citywide dropout rate of just 1.5 percent.

"But the teachers didn't believe it," Kimball told *60 Minutes*. "They knew it was cooking the books. They told me that. Parents told me that. The superintendent of schools would make the public believe it was one school. But it is in the system; it is in all of Houston."

Educators and experts consulted by *60 Minutes* put Houston's true dropout rate somewhere between 25 and 50 percent.

Administrators were incentivized to fudge the numbers. Before being named as President Bush's secretary of education, Rodney Paige was superintendent of Houston's schools, and he had instituted a policy of holding principals accountable for making goals in areas like dropout rates and test scores. Principals worked under one-year contracts, and those who met the goals got cash bonuses of up to five thousand dollars and other rewards. Those who fell short were transferred, demoted, or their contracts were not renewed.

The phony low dropout rates—in Houston and all of Texas— were one of the accomplishments then-Texas Governor George W. Bush cited when he campaigned to become the "education president."

How about test scores? Schools and their principals were judged on how well their students did on tests. In addition to its amazingly low dropout rates, Houston also won praise for raising the average scores on a statewide achievement test that was given to tenth graders.

But school officials were accused of distorting test scores by controlling who took the tests.

At Houston schools, Kimball said, principals raised average test scores by keeping low-performing kids from taking the test. That could be accomplished by keeping those kids from going from ninth grade—which had no test—to the tenth grade, where they'd be tested. If a kid passes every subject in ninth grade but fails algebra, the rational response is to say, "You can go to tenth grade, but you must retake ninth grade algebra." Instead, kids who had passed every subject except algebra were held back and forced to repeat ninth grade in its entirety.

Gilbert Moreno, who is the director of the Association for the Advancement of Mexican-Americans, told *60 Minutes* that many Houston high schools had bulging ninth grades and very small tenth grades. One school, he said, held back more than 60 percent of its ninth-graders. The only reason was to keep those kids from taking the test in tenth grade.

Another way to boost test scores is to cheat. As the years ticked by, rumors and reports of test score cheating perpetrated by teachers and administrators became more persistent. One of the most notorious cases involved the public school system in Atlanta, Georgia.

In October 2010, the Georgia Bureau of Investigation began visiting schools and talking to teachers. After more than two thousand interviews, the investigators concluded that forty-four schools had cheated on test scores and that a "culture of fear, intimidation and retaliation had infested the district, allowing cheating—at all levels—to go unchecked for years." They wrote that test score data had been "used as an abusive and cruel weapon to embarrass and punish." Several teachers reported to investigators that they had been given a choice: either make their test score targets or be placed on a Performance Development Plan, which was often a precursor to termination.

Righton Johnson, a lawyer with Balch & Bingham who sat in on some of the interviews, told *The New Yorker* that most Atlanta teachers—many of whom taught in the city's toughest and poorest schools—thought they were committing a victimless crime. "They didn't see the value in the test, so they didn't see that they were devaluing the kids by cheating," she said. Those who cheated viewed it as a practical solution to a hopeless problem, and something that needed to be done in order to focus on issues that were more relevant to their students' lives.

Test score cheating produced another and perhaps even more serious unintended consequence. A significant component of NCLB is the concept of adequate yearly progress (AYP). This means that if a school falsifies its students' test scores in one year, then during the second year—when those same students are now even further behind—it needs to *increase* its cheating efforts to ensure that scores are higher than the previous year's. At Parks Middle School, which became the "poster child" of NCLB cheating, Principal Christopher Waller told *The New Yorker* that the process of changing answers on tests had become "a well-oiled machine." Schools colluded with each other; for example, a principal at another elementary school in Atlanta emailed Waller confidential information from the Department of Education revealing the number of questions students in each grade needed to answer correctly in order to get a passing score. After every test session, Waller had a team of nine trusted teachers assemble in the chorus room, where they would carefully erase wrong answers and mark the correct ones.

In fact, the vast scheme was revealed only when the Georgia Governor's Office of Student Achievement discovered that tests from certain schools exhibited an excessive number of erasure marks, indicating an exceptional number of wrong answers had been corrected.

The pressure on low-income schools to produce ever-better scores was enormous. "There's a fallacy in the law and everybody knows it," said Alabama State Superintendent Joe Morton in 2010. According to NCLB, by 2014 every child was supposed to test on grade level in reading and math. "That can't happen," said Morton. "You have too many variables and you have too many scenarios, and everybody knows that would never happen."

In his book *Real Education*, libertarian author Charles Murray wrote of the law: "The United States Congress, acting with large bipartisan majorities, at the urging of the President, enacted as the law of the land that all children are to be above average." Perhaps it was an achievable goal in wealthy school districts, but impossible in many low-income districts.

With NCLB, the nation's education doctors once again prescribed expensive sugar pills; only these were unlike the old placebos of previous decades in that they were hard for school districts to swallow. So, like stubborn patients who don't like swallowing pills, schools and states endeavored to placate the doctor, pretended to take the medicine, and kept on doing what they always did, which was to focus on winning small day-to-day victories rather than tackling difficult and deep-rooted social and economic problems.

Eventually, even the federal government realized that NCLB was even worse than a placebo: it was actually damaging to schools in poor neighborhoods. In March 2011, CNN reported that Secretary of Education Arne Duncan estimated that four out of five schools in the United States would not make their NCLB benchmarks by the law's target year of 2014, and when the test scores were counted for the current school year, numbers could show that US schools were already at that failure rate.

He blamed the looming failure rate not on schools but on the law itself.

"This law has created dozens of ways for schools to fail and very few ways to help them succeed," Duncan told the House Committee on Education and the Workforce. "We should get out of the business of labeling schools as failures and create a new law that is fair and flexible, and focused on the schools and students most at risk."

Race to the Top and Common Core

The Great Recession hit America hard. Millions of people lost their jobs, homes went into foreclosure, banks and big corporations went bankrupt, and local tax revenues—which fund public schools—declined.

Across America, the feeling grew that Washington needed to *do something*—and it needed to be *big*.

One of the federal government's major responses was the American Recovery and Reinvestment Act of 2009 (ARRA), commonly referred to as the Stimulus or the Recovery Act. Enacted by the Congress in early 2009, it was promptly signed into law on February 17 of the same year by President Barack Obama.

The cost of the Recovery Act was estimated to be $787 billion at the time of passage, and later increased to $831 billion for the period of the decade following. The act included direct spending in infrastructure, education, health, and energy; federal tax incentives; and expansion of unemployment benefits and other social welfare provisions. It also created the President's Economic Recovery Advisory Board.

Race to the Top (also known variously as R2T, RTTT, or RTT) was the education component of the Recovery Act. It was allocated $4.35 billion in federal funding, to be distributed by the United States Department of Education under Secretary of Education Arne Duncan. The fund, created through the Recovery Act, was unique. No education secretary had ever had so much money for school improvement with so few conditions from Congress.

The goals of RTTT were to "encourage and reward States that are creating the conditions for education innovation and reform; and achieving significant improvement in student outcomes, including making substantial gains in student achievement, closing achievement gaps, improving high school graduation rates, and ensuring student preparation for success in college and careers."

Reform Areas

Within RTTT, the White House delineated five reform areas:

1. Designing and implementing rigorous standards and high-quality assessments, by encouraging states to work jointly toward a system of common academic standards that built toward college and career readiness, and that included improved assessments designed to measure critical knowledge and higher-order thinking skills.
2. Attracting and keeping great teachers and leaders in America's classrooms, by expanding effective support to teachers and principals; reforming and improving teacher preparation; revising teacher evaluation, compensation, and retention policies to encourage

and reward effectiveness; and working to ensure that the nation's most talented teachers were placed in the schools and subjects where they were needed the most.

3. Supporting data systems that informed decisions and improved instruction, by fully implementing a statewide longitudinal data system, assessing and using data to drive instruction, and making data more accessible to key stakeholders.

4. Using innovation and effective approaches to turn around struggling schools by asking states to prioritize and transform persistently low-performing schools.

5. Demonstrating and sustaining education reform by promoting collaborations between business leaders, educators, and other stakeholders to raise student achievement and close achievement gaps, and by expanding support for high-performing public charter schools, reinvigorating math and science education, and promoting other conditions favorable to innovation and reform.

Gone (at least in theory) was the notion of universal student testing that had been the centerpiece of No Child Left Behind and which had been despised by students, parents, educators, and politicians alike. However, as will be seen, the idea of universal testing snuck through the back door into RTTT with Common Core.

RTTT Scoring System

The structure of the program was unique. In the simplest terms, it was a competitive grant program structured like a contest.

States were awarded points for satisfying certain educational metrics, such as using performance-based evaluations for teachers and principals based on multiple measures of educator effectiveness, adopting common standards (though adoption of the Common Core State Standards was not required), building and using data systems, adopting policies that did not prohibit the expansion of high-quality charter schools, and turning around the lowest-performing schools. State applications for funding were scored on selection criteria worth a total of 500 points. Each metric (listed below) was worth a defined number of points. The goal was to get a perfect score of 500, or as close to it as possible. A perfect bid score of 500 points could be worth hundreds of millions of dollars in federal grants, depending upon the size of the state. The four largest states by population—California, New York, Texas, and Florida—were eligible for the largest grants.

Great Teachers and Leaders (138 total points)
- Improving teacher and principal effectiveness based on performance (58 points).
- Ensuring equitable distribution of effective teachers and principals (25 points).
- Providing high-quality pathways for aspiring teachers and principals (21 points).
- Providing effective support to teachers and principals (20 points).
- Improving the effectiveness of teacher and principal preparation programs (14 points).

State Success Factors (125 total points)
- Articulating State's education reform agenda and local education agencies' (LEAs) participation in it (65 points).

- Building strong statewide capacity to implement, scale up, and sustain proposed plans (30 points).
- Demonstrating significant progress in raising achievement and closing gaps (30 points).

Standards and Assessments (70 total points)
- Developing and adopting common standards (40 points).
- Supporting the transition to enhanced standards and high-quality assessments (20 points).
- Developing and implementing common, high-quality assessments (10 points).

General Selection Criteria (55 total points)
- Ensuring successful conditions for high-performing charters and other innovative schools (40 points).
- Making education funding a priority (10 points).
- Demonstrating other significant reform conditions (5 points).

Turning Around the Lowest-Achieving Schools (50 total points).
- Turning around the lowest-achieving schools (40 points).
- Intervening in the lowest-achieving schools and local education agencies (LEAs) (10 points).

Data Systems to Support Instruction (47 total points).
- Fully implementing a statewide longitudinal data system (24 points).
- Using data to improve instruction (18 points).
- Accessing and using State data (5 points).

In addition to the 485 possible points from the selection criteria above, applicants were assessed based on six priorities, including the prioritization of STEM (science, technology, engineering, and math) education. This was worth another fifteen points for a possible total of 500.

The data system provision became significant because to enable teacher evaluations for "improving teacher and principal effectiveness based on performance," schools needed to track student performance in all grades, which was a euphemism for the kind of comprehensive testing regime that made many parents and students cringe but that the reformers argued was necessary for any serious attempt to track not only student progress but also teacher effectiveness.

Timetable

Like most other grant programs, states had to apply by a deadline. Three sets of deadlines were set, called "phases." They were:

Phase 1: Applications for funding were due on January 19, 2010. Forty states and the District of Columbia applied for funding. On March 29, 2010, the two Phase 1 winners were announced—Delaware (awarded $100 million) and Tennessee (awarded $500 million).

Phase 2: The application deadline was June 1, 2010. On August 24, 2010, the winners were announced—nine states and Washington, DC.

Phase 3: Only states that had lost in Phases 1 and 2 were eligible for Phase 3. Applications were split into two parts. Part I was due November 22, 2011, and Part II was due December 16. Seven more states were winners.

Over three rounds, eighteen states plus the District of Columbia were awarded grants totaling $4.1 billion. Alaska, North Dakota, Texas, and Vermont did not submit Race to the Top applications in any phase. A related program was Race to the Top—Early Learning Challenge, jointly conducted by the Department of Education and the United States Department of Health and Human Services. The RTT-ELC grant competition focused on improving early learning and development programs for young children.

The first RTT–ELC competition was held in 2011 and awarded grants to nine states: California, Delaware, Maryland, Massachusetts, Minnesota, North Carolina, Ohio, Rhode Island, and Washington.

In 2012, the next five highest-rated states from the first round received funding: Colorado, Illinois, New Mexico, Oregon, and Wisconsin.

In 2013, RTT-ELC grants went to Georgia, Kentucky, Michigan, New Jersey, Pennsylvania, and Vermont.

Judging

Anyone who researches RTTT will soon ask themselves an important question: Who judged the applications? Who decided which states would receive hundreds of millions of dollars and which states would receive nothing?

In 2010 the state of Colorado tried to find out—and couldn't. Five judges had read and scored Colorado's application, which came in too low for funding. For its months of grant writing effort, the state got nothing. The identities of the five judges remained secret.

As the *Denver Post* reported on November 11, 2011, Colorado state officials felt at least one reviewer unfairly treated the state's failed application for federal Race to the Top grant money, but the public will never know who it was.

In September 2010 the newspaper sent a formal request to the US Department of Education asking for the names of the five panelists who had reviewed Colorado's application in the second round of competition for $4 billion in education stimulus money.

Colorado—which many believed would be among the top finishers in the Race to the Top competition—had received a final score of 420 on a scale of 500 points. This was the average of five scores from five reviewers. Out of nineteen finalists, Colorado ended up near the bottom, at number seventeen. This caused it to lose out on $175 million in federal RTTT funds.

Comments on Colorado's application ranged from glowing to critical. But two of the five reviewers gave the application particularly low marks. One scored Colorado the lowest among all nineteen finalists with 339 points, repeatedly citing lack of union support, "which weakens the likelihood of widespread impact."

Former Lt. Gov. Barbara O'Brien, who had led the state's Race to the Top effort, said that when state officials appeared for an oral interview session about the application, at least two reviewers had appeared to have already decided against Colorado.

"It was sickening to have tried so hard and to walk in and you can tell by just looking at two of the five judges that they weren't receptive to our case," she told the *Denver Post*.

During that round, both Colorado and Louisiana were knocked out of the competition despite widespread belief they had strong applications to win their share of RTTT funding.

Many analysts argued that the names of reviewers who judged each state's applications should be released. But it hasn't happened yet.

In December 2012, Colorado managed to win $17.9 million in Phase 3 funding for early childhood education programs. Five states had been eligible for the money in the second round of funding for the Race to the Top: Early Learning Challenge. The first round of early childhood funding in 2011 had awarded money to nine of thirty-seven applicants. The second round allowed the five next-highest finishers to modify their applications for a smaller share of money. All five, including Colorado, were awarded up to half of their original request.

The Race to Get Federal Funds

Money brings leverage, and school budgets are perennially tight. How much leverage does the federal government have? As the American Association of School Administrators wrote in *School Budgets 101*, "The school budget involves many different individuals and entities across several levels of government... School budget resources come from a combination of local, state and federal contributions. The 2006—07 school year is the most recent year for which we have a full tabulation of the education funding contributions split between local government (43.9 percent), state government (47.6 percent) and federal government (8.5 percent)."

Like it or not, despite the fact that federal funds typically account for a much smaller fraction of funding than either state or local sources, they're enough to make most school administrators sit up and take notice. Indeed, the whole point of a federal grant to a school is to get the school or state to bend toward federal requirements. Most states accept the deal, but no state is required to. Indeed, in January 2010, Governor Rick Perry announced that Texas would not compete for up to $700 million in federal education money. He called Race to the Top an unacceptable intrusion on states' control over education.

RTTT had proposed nineteen federal "priorities" that states seeking RTTT funds would be required to address. Few of the priorities entailed structural changes; instead, they primarily emphasized things like professional development, "building strong statewide capacity," ensuring an "equitable distribution" of good teachers and principals, "making education funding a priority," and so on. And, in a move that created pressure to adopt standards, states could instantly collect three of the nineteen priorities by promising to adopt the Common Core and its federally funded tests.

A complex and labor-intensive application process drove Race to the Top, and most states were all too happy to make the attempt. The procedure was so cumbersome that, as *Education Week* reported, the Bill & Melinda Gates Foundation hand-picked fifteen states to receive up to $250,000 each to hire consultants to help them fill out their applications. McKinsey & Co. and the Bridgespan Group were two examples of blue-chip consulting firms used by states. The "Chosen 15" states were: Arkansas, Arizona, Florida, Georgia, Kentucky, Louisiana, Massachusetts, Minnesota, New Mexico, New York, North Carolina, Ohio, Pennsylvania, Tennessee, and Texas. A month later, the Gates Foundation offered assistance to the remaining thirty-five states if they met eight education reform criteria that mirrored the criteria by which the US Department of Education had proposed judging applications for aid under the education-reform competition. In June 2011, the US General Accounting Office issued a report entitled "Race to the Top: Reform Efforts Are Under Way and Information Sharing Could Be Improved." The report stated, "Officials in the twenty states we interviewed told us that applying for RTTT required a significant amount of time and effort. Many officials we interviewed estimated spending thousands of hours to prepare the RTTT application; however, they generally did not track the total costs associated with their efforts. One state official estimated that her state spent at least 4,000 hours preparing their RTTT application. Also, all states we interviewed received grants to hire consultants who helped prepare the RTTT applications. For example, the Bill and Melinda Gates Foundation reported funding technical assistance providers who assisted 25 states in developing their RTTT applications. Each of these 25 states, including fourteen of the twenty we interviewed, received consulting services worth $250,000 with these funds. With grants such as these, states hired consultants who provided a range of services, including drafting material for the application and conducting background research and analysis. State officials told us that consulting firms received between $75,000 and $620,000 for their services. According to US Department of Education officials, states commonly receive external support to apply for federal grants, such as the Teacher Incentive Fund, in an effort to leverage their resources more effectively. However, Department of Education officials also explained that the RTTT competition was more comprehensive in scope than other federal discretionary grants, which may have prompted states to seek out a greater level of external support."

Money Now, Results Later

Race to the Top funds were awarded on the basis of *future plans*, not *present results*. Rushing to meet program deadlines, states cobbled together proposals loaded with promises. States promised to adopt "clear, content-rich, sequenced, spiraled, detailed curricular frameworks" and "scalable and sustained strategies for turning around clusters of low-performing schools." Applications ran to hundreds of densely worded pages, making the process heavily dependent on grant-writing skills. Critics charged that some of the dozen winning states were actually below average on the progressive reforms that Race to the Top was supposedly seeking to promote.

In seeking to throw the initiative for reform back to the states, the program perhaps unwittingly placed an emphasis on promises rather than accomplishments. Race to the Top offered an ambiguous scoring criteria and a vague process for selecting and training judges. The reliance of winning states on grant writers and outside consultants also meant that the commitment of key civic leaders, legislators, and education officials to the promised reform agenda may have been weak.

In 2012, the Center for American Progress (CAP) published "Race to the Top: What Have We Learned from the States So Far?" The report, which was generally favorable to RTTT, said, in part, "In some states, there's been little collaboration between key stakeholders, and states could do more to communicate reforms... Every state has delayed some part of their grant implementation, and some observers worry about a lack of capacity... One Florida reporter said, 'Only a handful of districts feel like they're prepared to do [new teacher evaluations]. Most feel like they're rushing.' Some states will most likely not accomplish all of the goals outlined in their grants. The goals that many of the states outlined in their applications are very high... States and districts very rarely, if ever, have reached such high achievement benchmarks, and it's almost certain that some of the states will not meet their goals."

In 2013 the Economic Policy Institute published "Mismatches in Race to the Top Limit Educational Improvement: Lack of Time, Resources, and Tools to Address Opportunity Gaps Puts Lofty State Goals Out of Reach." The report said:

> "This assessment draws three main conclusions about Race to the Top after three years:
> "1. States made unrealistic and impossible promises...
> "2. RTTT policies fall short on teacher improvement and fail to address core drivers of opportunity gaps...
> "3. RTTT shortcomings have spurred state–district and union–management conflicts that hinder progress."

For example, in January 2011 the state of Ohio was awarded a $400 million RTTT grant to be spent over four years. According to NPR, Ohio's ambitious plan called for the state by 2014 to:

- Increase the high school graduation rate by two percentage points to 88 percent.
- Reduce by half the gaps between white and non-white students' graduation rates.
- Reduce by half performance gaps between white and non-white students on state and national assessments.
- Reduce by half the gaps between Ohio and top-performing states on national reading and math assessments.

- Double the projected increase in college enrollment for
  students age 19 and younger.

In the spring of 2015, the *Columbus Dispatch* wrote, "Four
years and $400 million later, Ohio has met one of five goals for
the federal Race to the Top grant program. The state... fell short
of reducing achievement gaps for minority students, improving
reading and math scores as compared with the best-performing
states, and increasing college enrollment. Although most goals
were not achieved, state education officials focused on the positive
in their final Race to the Top report." Ohio still received its full
complement of federal Race to the Top funds.

Federal RTTT funds were almost never withheld from any
state for nonperformance. As Drew University political scientist
Patrick McGuinn wrote in "Stimulating Reform: Race to the Top,
Competitive Grants and the Obama Education Agenda," "It is
one thing for RTTT to secure promises of state action, another
thing for states to deliver promised action, and another thing
entirely for their action to result in improvements in educational
outcomes."

Common Core, which began as a collaborative effort among
states, became a quasi-federal initiative with lots of reluctant
participants. In pushing states to hurriedly adopt new evaluation
systems that specifically used test results to gauge teachers, RTTT
ensured that many flimsy systems would be quickly rolled out
and interwoven with the Common Core and its associated tests.

In the rush to *do something*, the infrastructure to effectively
implement RTTT often didn't exist. Criteria for who should judge
and how they should do so were hurriedly created, and, as we saw
in the case of Colorado, the judging process was not transparent.

Race to the Top used funds and public pressure to induce states to promise to adopt a slate of prescriptions. In many places, this led to a rushed adoption and ensured that many policies were executed poorly, undermining public confidence and support. That is a poor strategy for prompting innovation or improvement. The public imagination is often captured by the fact of a federal program that promises to *do something*, but what matters is how such programs actually work.

Common Core

As we have seen, throughout American history the recurring political impulse has been to *do something* about schools while resisting any suggestion that the federal government insert itself into school curriculums at any level. *What* children are taught and *how* they are taught has been turf jealously guarded by the states. No politician ever got elected on a promise to create national curriculum standards. There's some nuance here, though; some federal efforts, including No Child Left Behind, have established national *testing* standards, which many conservatives viewed as a backdoor way for Washington to take over education from the states.

Yet among many academic and industrial professionals, the idea of national curriculum standards has long been embraced as a worthy goal. For them, it makes no sense for children in different states to go to school with varying levels of expectation and support.

In the wake of the Great Recession the cry went up to *do something*, which, since the days of Sputnik, had always happened when the public felt that the nation's schools were not producing qualified students. Elementary and high school education became part of the national to-do list. The Obama administration chose not to double down on the NCLB federal testing standards that had been judged a failure and which would be resisted by state politicians, but to take a different approach with Race to the Top.

Conveniently, the effort to develop a national set of standards had already begun outside of the Beltway. A 2004 report from the American Diploma Project entitled *Ready or Not: Creating a High School Diploma That Counts* had stated that high schools were not adequately preparing students for either college or employment. The solution to this problem, said the ADP, was a common set of rigorous standards.

It was state leaders, including governors and state commissioners of education from forty-eight states, two territories, and the District of Columbia, who in 2008 began working to create this common set of standards through the National Governors Association Center for Best Practices (NGA Center) and the Council of Chief State School Officers (CCSSO). Governors and state school chiefs launched the effort to ensure all students, regardless of where they lived, were graduating from high school with a common platform of knowledge and training.

Liberal philanthropists joined the cause. The Gates Foundation and the Bill and Melinda Gates Foundation provided $35 million to the effort for purposes of developing and implementing a new education system in the United States. The plan came to be called the Common Core State Standards Initiative (CCSSI), and was published in June 2009.

Meanwhile, in February 2009, President Obama signed the American Recovery and Reinvestment Act (the Stimulus Bill) into law, which created and funded Race to the Top, in which states had to "commit" to adopting common standards.

While the government did not explicitly name Common Core or any other set of standards, states that agreed to implement Common Core got higher scores in their quest for Race to the Top funds.

Within two months of their release, the Common Core State Standards had been adopted by twenty-eight states that promised to implement the standards by fall 2013 and by the 2014–15 school year replace their existing state assessments with tests aligned to the Common Core. By the end of 2010, a total of forty-one states and the District of Columbia had agreed to implement the Common Core. Five more states, four territories, and the Department of Defense Education Activity adopted the Common Core in 2011.

Backers praised this rapid acceptance, saying that Common Core would restore those state standards that had been lowered in response to No Child Left Behind.

Some states, including Virginia and Texas, chose to write their own standards rather than adopt Common Core. In doing so, both states were still eligible to apply for Race to the Top funds. Texas did not submit an application, and Virginia applied but was not awarded any money.

In a January 13, 2010, letter to Secretary of Education Arne Duncan, Texas Governor Rick Perry explained why Texas would not be applying for Race to the Top funds.

"In the interest of preserving our state sovereignty over matters concerning education and shielding local schools from unwarranted federal intrusion into local district decision-making, Texas will not be submitting an application for RTTT funds." He then provided political cover for himself by citing the costs of adopting Common Core standards: "Adopting national standards and tests would also require the purchase of new textbooks, assessments, and professional development tools, costing Texas taxpayers an estimated $3 billion, on top of the billions of dollars of Texas has already invested in developing our strong standards. In a state with 4.7 million students, this amounts to more than $635 per student, many times what Texas is eligible for under the U.S. Department of Education's RTTT funding guidelines."

State leaders in Kentucky, on the other hand, were so convinced of the merits of Common Core that they adopted them even before the standards were finalized in June 2010.

Governor Perry's letter echoed a growing objection to Common Core: that it was a financial windfall for textbook publishers and software developers.

Fox News reported that states would spend up to an estimated $10 billion up front, then as much as $800 million per year for the first seven years that the program was up and running. While much of the cost would be on new, Common Core–aligned textbooks and curriculum, added expenses would include teacher training, technology upgrades, testing, and assessment.

For example, in a report released in January 2014, education officials in Maryland estimated that it would require $100 million to upgrade computers statewide to support the testing that was the centerpiece of Common Core. California and Georgia also reported a high cost to implementing Common Core, with the former estimated to spend approximately $35 million per year, or about thirty dollars per student, in testing costs alone.

Common Core advocates responded by pointing out that items like textbooks, study materials, and information technology were expected to depreciate, and upgrades had to be funded whether they were done under the umbrella of Common Core or any other program. Analysts estimated that schools were already spending nearly $700 million per year testing and assessing students, and that many of the new expenses were not much more than what schools would be spending anyway.

Even so, as the program deepened, the political complaints about the cost mounted, and provided conservative politicians like Rick Perry a convenient target that everyone hated: More spending heaped on the backs of state taxpayers.

Representative Blaine Luetkemeyer of Missouri told Fox News, "When first promoting Common Core State Standards, the Department of Education used a carrot-and-stick approach by awarding grant money and waivers from No Child Left Behind regulations in exchange for adoption of the standards. At a time of economic recession and shrinking state budgets, this federal money enticed the vast majority of states to adopt CCSSI and their aligned assessments, often without states being able to fully analyze the future costs of annual testing. I'm afraid the bloom is off the rose as Missouri, and a number of other states, are realizing the new assessments will cost nearly twice as much as the previous state-based tests. Moreover, I am concerned that many of our rural districts will not even have the technological capability required for the new tests, adding even more costs."

How much of this talk was reality and how much was pure politics (that is, "Whatever Democratic president Barack Obama supports, we Republicans are against")? It's hard to say. The Common Core standards were developed by an association of state governors operating outside of the nation's capital. The standards were then embraced by the US Department of Education and states were encouraged—but not required—to adopt them. Therefore a politician could take either side and find political cover.

In not just red states, however, Common Core was met with resistance. At a board meeting in January 2014, the New York State United Teachers union pushed back against the Common Core curriculum standards. The teachers' union withdrew its support of Common Core and cast a vote of "no confidence" in the state's education commissioner John King Jr., calling for his removal. Union president Richard C. Iannuzzi said in a statement on the group's website:

"Educators understand that introducing new standards, appropriate curriculum, and meaningful assessments are ongoing aspects of a robust educational system. These are complex tasks made even more complex when attempted during a time of devastating budget cuts. The implementation plan in New York State has failed. The commissioner has pursued policies that repeatedly ignore the voices of parents and educators who have identified problems and called on him to move more thoughtfully. Instead of listening to and trusting parents and teachers to know and do what's right for students, the commissioner has offered meaningless rhetoric and token change. Instead of making the major course corrections that are clearly needed, including backing a three-year moratorium on high-stakes consequences for students and teachers from state testing, he has labeled everyone and every meaningful recommendation as distractions."

The union had been "sounding warning bells since 2011," NYSUT vice president Maria Neira said in the statement, criticizing the overemphasis on standardized testing, a rushed timeline for implementation, and unrealistic assessments for Common Core state standards.

Regardless of your political affiliation, it would be difficult to deny that both NCLB and Common Core represented a windfall in profits for publishers of educational materials.

For example, millions in Race to the Top funding went to two large groups of states that had banded together, ostensibly to save money.

One was the Smarter Balanced Assessment Consortium, a public agency supported by fifteen states, one territory, and the Bureau of Indian Affairs. Smarter Balanced created an online assessment system aligned to the Common Core State Standards, as well as tools for educators to improve teaching and learning. Smarter Balanced is housed at UCLA's Graduate School of Education & Information Studies (GSE&IS).

The other was the Partnership for Assessment of Readiness for College and Careers, or PARCC, a group of eleven states working together to develop a modern assessment that replaces previous state standardized tests.

Those groups in turn paid vendors to develop Common Core testing and related materials for their members. According to numbers compiled by *Education Week*, the biggest chunk of federal dollars went to Apollo Global Management–owned McGraw-Hill ($72.5 million from Smarter Balanced), UK-based Pearson Education ($63 million from PARCC), and nonprofit Educational Testing Services ($42 million combined from both groups).

Pearson Education is a British-owned education publishing and assessment service to schools and corporations, as well as directly to students. Pearson owns educational media brands including Addison-Wesley, Peachpit, Prentice Hall, eCollege, Longman, Poptropica, and others.

As *Politico* reported in February 2015, aside from distributing the TV game show *Family Feud*, Pearson had made few inroads in the United States until it announced plans in the summer of 2000 to spend $2.5 billion on an American testing company.

The investment turned out to be a very smart move.

The next year, Congress passed the No Child Left Behind Act, which mandated millions of new standardized tests for millions of children in public schools. Pearson Education was poised to capitalize on the opportunity. The company expanded rapidly, taking advantage of many subsequent reform trends from online learning to the Common Core standards that were adopted in more than forty states. The company quickly reaped the benefits: of its eight billion dollars in annual global sales, half came from its North American education division.

But were US students or taxpayers well served?

Every time the nation faces a crisis—real or imagined—our system of education falls under the spotlight. Ever since Sputnik, American parents, politicians, and educators have periodically demanded *action*. Politicians have raced to promote one fix after another: new standards, new tests, new classroom technology, new profitable partnerships with the private sector.

In this atmosphere of crisis, a company like Pearson promises solutions. To beleaguered schools it sells the latest and trendiest education materials. It's no corporate lightweight; it calls itself the world's leading learning company. Its website—accessed in October 2015—touts heartwarming success stories such as this one:

"Mt. Ephraim School District, a small district located in Camden County, New Jersey, just across the Delaware river from Philadelphia, hired Leslie Koller to be the new superintendent in January 2013. Koller was charged with addressing declining rigor in classrooms, low teacher morale, and new state requirements. And because the Common Core assessments were scheduled for 2014–2015, she had a year to turn the district around.

"'When the 2013–14 school year started, I launched a communication plan to parents, teachers, and students,' said Koller. 'Parents were used to many of their children making honor roll. I told them that we were purchasing new curricula that were correlated to the common core State Standards. The first year we were purchasing a new language arts program and the following year we would purchase new math curriculum. I warned them that the new language arts program, Pearson's Reading Street, was very rigorous and that students would be facing more challenges this year.'"

The results? According to Pearson Education, student growth was seen at every grade level: "'Before Reading Street and common core, we celebrated the two or three students who exited kindergarten as readers. Now, we are celebrating an entire class of readers,' said kindergarten teacher Terri Bergin."

While Pearson Education may tout its products as being catalysts for change, such anecdotal evidence can't be taken as conclusive. After all, it may have been the presence of a new school superintendent that made the difference. But as part of Pearson PLC, a for-profit company with revenues of over $7 billion per year, Pearson Education will not hesitate to extoll the virtues of its products.

As a full service Common Core operation, not only does Pearson provide the assessments but it delivers textbooks, test prep material, and online support. It also produces the PARCC (Partnership for Assessment of Readiness for College and Careers) tests that are administered by a consortium of a dozen states and the District of Columbia.

Thanks to Presidents Bush and Obama, big money was to be made by the education testing and publishing industry. As the *Wall Street Journal* and the Thomas Fordham Institute revealed, the national cost for compliance with the Common Core standards was as high as eight billion dollars—and the profits would go almost directly to publishers of education materials. Peter Cohen, CEO of Pearson's K–12 division, boasted, "It's a really big deal. The Common Core standards are affecting literally every part of the business we're involved in." In an annual report to investors, Pearson showcased how it provided tests to twenty-three states and also developed the online application for Common Core mandated assessments in a total of forty-five states. James Mason, a PARCC state leader who helped negotiate the contract with Pearson, told *Education Week* that depending on a "number of factors," the Pearson contract with PARCC was of an "unprecedented scale."

After All the Spending, Still the Problems Remain

Aside from the profit motive, critics of Common Core for elementary and preschool children charged that the program did not address the root problems of education in low-income areas. Nancy Carlsson-Paige of Lesley University in Cambridge, a senior advisor to Defending the Early Years, a nonprofit project of the Survival Education Fund, Inc., wrote, "The adoption of CCSS falsely implies that making children learn these standards will combat the impact of poverty on development and learning, and create equal educational opportunity for all children.

"The United States is the wealthiest nation in the world and has the highest child poverty rate among industrialized nations. Corporate-style reformers would have us believe that we can solve the problem of poverty by mandating the teaching of basic skills in our nation's schools. But schools cannot solve all of the problems created by societal factors that exist outside of school walls. While we do not have all the answers, years of research tell us that schools, while important, cannot solve all the disadvantages created by poverty. In fact, during the last decade of 'education reform'—increased standards and testing, more accountability and data gathering—the inequalities in our education system have increased and the child poverty rate has grown."

A 2013 report by Elaine Weiss of the Broader, Bolder Approach to Education (BBA) organization entitled "Mismatches in Race to the Top Limit Educational Improvement" cited a lack of time, resources, and tools to address opportunity gaps that put lofty state goals out of reach.

The report, published three years after RTTT began and one year before funding ended, asserted that many states were behind schedule in meeting goals for improving instruction and school and educational outcomes. The challenges that states encountered holding schools and teachers accountable under the current standards were likely to grow as demands increased while time, staffing, and other resources remained flat or were further diminished.

The assessment drew three main conclusions about Race to the Top after three years:

- To win funding, states made unrealistic and impossible promises. Most grantee states promised to raise student achievement and close achievement gaps to an extent that would be impossible even with much longer timelines and larger funding boosts.
  The report found that virtually every state had to delay

implementation of its teacher evaluation systems, due to insufficient time to develop rubrics, pilot new systems, and/or train evaluators and others.

- RTTT policies fell short on teacher improvement and failed to address core drivers of opportunity gaps. "Districts heavily serving low-income and minority students, especially large urban districts, face some of the most severe challenges," said the report. "Tight timelines and lack of resources compound RTTT's failure to address poverty-related impediments to learning. Heightened pressure on districts to produce impossible gains from an overly narrow policy agenda has made implementation difficult and often counterproductive."

- RTTT shortcomings spurred state/district and union/ management conflicts that hindered progress. The heavy focus on evaluation and punishment over improvement made teachers, principals, and superintendents suspicious, and reduced support for RTTT.

Overall, the assessment found that the key tenet of Race to the Top—that states hold their teachers and schools accountable before helping them establish foundations for success—was deeply flawed. The push to do too much too quickly with too few resources led teachers, principals, and superintendents to express frustration and stress.

Most critically, the report stated that many of the major problems limiting student and school success remained unaddressed.

Doesn't that sound familiar? Haven't we seen over and over again that that impulse to improve schools fails to tackle the more significant underlying social and economic problems that are at the root of school failure for many low-income children? Race to the Top mirrored many of the components of— and suffered from many of the same flaws as—No Child Left Behind. Like its predecessor, RTTT relied heavily on test scores to evaluate teachers, principals, and entire schools, and it drew on a narrow set of policy strategies to reach ambitious goals of raising student achievement and closing gaps.

The 1983 report, *A Nation at Risk*, concluded that low achievement and large gaps threatened US competitiveness, and it championed reforms based on standards and accountability. Proponents of this approach blamed low achievement on the schools themselves: weak academic standards, lack of accountability, and insufficient competition within the education system. Subsequent presidents and their secretaries of education, as well as many governors, have embraced this strategy, which has been politically acceptable on both sides of the aisle. Even conservatives have been willing to put federal money directly into schools, a strategy that carries the implicit message of individual accountability: "If you can't succeed at a federally funded school, then it's *your* fault. We give you the school; all you have to do is show up and do the work." Anyone who has spent time in low-income areas knows that the reality of life in the neighborhood isn't that simple.

Long-term data from the National Assessment of Educational Progress (NAEP) suggest that the billions of dollars spent on schools during the past fifty years have not appreciably boosted achievement, and that income-based gaps have actually grown.

Evidence continues to mount that the problems reflected in schools have their roots beyond the front door of the schoolhouse. The impulse to *do something* at the visible level has not worked because we continually treat the symptoms of the problem, not the problems themselves. While the endless dispensing of billion-dollar sugar pills may make politicians feel as though they've taken action, we've seen over and over again that the patient keeps coming back with the same impairments. It's a cycle of ineffectiveness that needs to be broken.

PART TWO: SCHOOL REFORM— WHERE WE ARE NOW

The Latest Sputnik Moment: Waiting for Superman

In every generation a dramatic event or report gets the attention of the public and politicians, and the cry is heard across the land to *do something.*

The original Sputnik moment came in October 1957. In response to the Soviet space accomplishment, the nation resolved to *do something.* A year later, the National Defense Education Act was passed by Congress and signed into law by President Eisenhower.

The 1962 publication of Michael Harrington's *The Other America*, which revealed to middle-class folks the depth of poverty in America, again ignited public debate on the issue. In his State of the Union address on January 8, 1964, President Lyndon Johnson declared "War on Poverty." He said, "Our aim is not only to relieve the symptoms of poverty, but to cure it and, above all, to prevent it." A cornerstone of the War on Poverty was the Elementary and Secondary Education Act (ESEA), which Johnson signed into law on April 9, 1965. It was the most expansive federal education bill ever enacted.

In 1983, President Ronald Reagan's National Commission on Excellence in Education published *A Nation at Risk: The*

Imperative for Educational Reform, which asserted that American schools were failing. According to tests conducted in the 1970s, "American students were never first or second and, in comparison with other industrialized nations, were last seven times." The gloom-and-doom report ignited a new outcry for local, state, and federal reforms. As for President Reagan, one of his campaign promises had been to shut down the US Department of Education. Once elected, he never carried out his stated plan. Instead he did nothing—he championed no federal education program and no program to combat poverty.

During the 1988 US presidential campaign, candidate George H. W. Bush announced, "I want to be the education president. I want to lead a renaissance of quality in our schools." Having won the White House, in late September 1989 President Bush called the nation's governors to a high-level summit in Charlottesville, Virginia, to discuss the problem of education. The gathering was to be the catalyst for standards-based education accountability. But in the four years of his term in office, Bush, like Reagan before him, did nothing to attack the challenge of how to educate low-income children.

The election of Democrat Bill Clinton in 1992 marked a return to federal activism in education. For those who wanted the federal government to *do something*, Clinton was ready to deliver. Clinton spearheaded two efforts: Goals 2000: The Educate America Act, and the renewal of ESEA, which was renamed Improving America's Schools Act, or IASA. Once again the federal money spigot opened. The doctor prescribed expensive sugar pills designed to make politicians feel better, but ultimately had little effect on the students.

April 1998 saw the publication of yet another official report. The US Department of Education published *Achievement in the United States: Progress Since "A Nation at Risk"?* Authored by Pascal D. Forgione Jr., PhD, the US commissioner of education statistics, the report painted a gloomy picture of education in America.

In 2001, Texas Governor George W. Bush took up residence in the White House. Unlike his father George H. W. Bush, the younger Bush was ready to *do something* about education. No Child Left Behind (NCLB) quickly made its way through Congress with bipartisan support, including from Democratic Senator Edward Kennedy. President Bush signed it into law on January 8, 2002. Billions were earmarked for states that set their own standards of education—and tested the kids to ensure they measured up. Eventually, NCLB came to be regarded by both educators and politicians as an underfunded, overmandated failure.

The year 2008 saw the entrance of President Barack Obama. His foray into the *do something* arena took the form of Race to the Top. As part of the overall American Recovery and Reinvestment Act, RTTT was allocated $4.35 billion in federal funding, to be distributed by the United States Department of Education under Secretary of Education Arne Duncan. Ultimately, Race to the Top relied heavily on test scores to evaluate teachers, principals, and schools, and the billions in funding seemed to primarily benefit commercial providers of education materials.

Waiting for Superman

The nation's next Sputnik moment came in 2010 with the release of a documentary film followed by a companion book.

Waiting for Superman, the effort of director Davis Guggenheim and producer Lesley Chilcott, offered a critique of the American public education system by following several public school students as they hoped to be accepted into a charter school. The movie premiered at the 2010 Sundance Film Festival and took home the Audience Award for Best US Documentary.

In the film's loose plot, Geoffrey Canada—American educator, social activist, and president of the Harlem Children's Zone in Harlem—describes his journey as an educator and the shock he felt when he realized that Superman was a fictional character and that no single person was powerful enough to save society. He extends this idea to the nation's public school systems and suggests that there's no "Superman" who is going to fix it. (It's not exactly clear who among us believes that a Superman will save our schools; while it captures the imagination, the metaphor seems fuzzy.) Meanwhile, in the film, five kids— Anthony, Bianca, Daisy, Emily, and Francisco—want to get a good education and go to college. With the odds against them, the five see their only hope as winning the lottery for a coveted spot in a charter school. The film provided a strong emotional hook; from different perspectives, the children's stories were hopeful, fascinating, and heartbreaking.

Neither the director nor the producer were educators; Davis Guggenheim had directed a wide variety of films, including a biography of the rock band U2, while Lesley Chilcott was a film producer and director known for *An Inconvenient Truth* (2006) and *It Might Get Loud* (2008).

The initial spark that inspired director Davis Guggenheim is revealing.

As Guggenheim told the Christian Broadcasting Network (CBN.com), "I was originally offered to make the movie, and I actually said 'no.' I thought that the subject of education was too complicated. The next morning I was packing my kids up in my minivan and taking them to school with juice boxes and backpacks. Out of the corner of my eye, I started to see the local public schools that I was driving by. And it started to haunt me that my kids whom I send to private school were having a great education, but the kids in my own neighborhood were not. I said, 'Well, maybe that is the approach that I should make for this movie. What if I made a movie that was about the kids?' and said, 'Why can't we give every kid that great education?'"

When a system is troubled—as is our system of education—it's possible that a fresh vision offered by someone outside the system could provide new insights. The other side of the coin is that someone with no experience in the trenches of real-life low-income education, and whose kids attend private schools, might resort to simply restating familiar, worn-out themes.

Evidence suggests that instead of approaching the subject with an open mind, the filmmakers set out to validate the same agenda that has been offered over and over again by those who want to *do something* to "fix" our nation's public schools. This mindset included the film's financial backers. The people who paid for the film got what they wanted: an affirmation of the same approach that has been tried in the past without effect.

In the arena of funding for public school education reform, three powerful private foundations—the Bill and Melinda Gates Foundation, the Eli and Edythe Broad Foundation, and the Walton Family Foundation—dominate the field. Regardless of the nuances that differentiate their motivations, the goals of the Big Three for reshaping public education are in alignment: deregulation, school choice, competition among schools, teacher accountability, and data-based decision making. To achieve their goals they support and fund the same strategies: charter schools, standardized testing for students, merit pay for teachers, closing schools and firing teachers when scores aren't high enough, and extensive data collection on the performance of every student and teacher. The Gates Foundation contributed $2 million for marketing *Waiting for Superman*, which was in perfect alignment with the foundation's mission of promoting charter schools and testing.

Dire Warnings

Waiting for Superman reached the same conclusion that was promoted by *A Nation at Risk* in 1983, but even more powerfully because it was a film that anyone could watch. With a broad brush it condemned the American public education system. It painted a picture of powerful teachers' unions and administrators who couldn't fire a teacher who was tenured. Teaching standards were called into question, and statistical comparisons made between different types of primary or secondary educational institutions: public school, private school, and charter school. There were also comparisons made between schools in affluent neighborhoods versus schools in low-income areas. Since charter schools do not operate with the same restrictions as public institutions, they were depicted as having a better chance of educating students.

The film didn't scrimp on statistics, and introduced a carefully chosen array of education-related numbers designed to show how poorly the public school system was performing.

The viewer was told that in 2006, 69% of eighth-graders scored below proficient in reading and 68% scored below proficient in math. Colorful graphs showed dismal American performance as compared to that of other nations, as well as mediocre American student progress over time. Among thirty developed countries in 2006, the viewer was told that while the US placed fifth in terms of K–12 spending per student, we placed 25th in terms of math scores. And despite the massive increase in per-pupil education spending in the US from 1971 to 2006, a national test for reading suggested that no change in academic performance was recorded from 1971 to 2004. High school graduation rates for minorities were barely 60 percent. The majority of prison inmates were high school dropouts.

Waiting for Superman asserted the familiar refrain that the US was "not producing large numbers of scientists and doctors in this country anymore… This means we are not only less educated, but also less economically competitive."

The reality of public school performance is far more nuanced. Those who seek to "fix" our public schools repeat the familiar assertion that US public schools are failing and our students trail far behind their peers in other nations. On a macro level, the claims are groundless. You have to drill down to find the truth: where it exists, which is *not* everywhere, the root of poor achievement is poverty.

For example, since 2001 the International Association for the Evaluation of Educational Achievement (IEA), an international organization of national research institutions and governmental research agencies has conducted the "Progress in International Reading Literacy Study (PIRLS)." The most recent report is from 2011. In that year, fifty-seven education systems (including countries and other education systems) participated in PIRLS, with fifty-three having participated at the fourth-grade level. Findings of the reading achievement of fourth-grade students in 2011 included:

* The overall reading average scale score for US students (556) was higher than the international PIRLS scale average, which was set to 500.

* In 2011, the United States was among the top thirteen education systems (five education systems had higher averages and seven were not measurably different). The United States average was higher than forty education systems.

* The five education systems with average scores above the US average were Hong Kong-CHN, Florida-USA (which entered as a separate school system), the Russian Federation, Finland, and Singapore.

* Compared with 2001, the US average score was 14 points higher in 2011 (542 in 2001 vs. 556 in 2011).

* Compared with 2006, the US average score was 16 points higher in 2011 (540 in 2006 vs. 556 in 2001).

It's a fair question to ask if all public schools in America scored the same. They did not. Generally, schools in wealthier school districts performed better than schools in low-income districts. One way of determining the relative wealth of a school district is to measure how many students are eligible for free or reduced-price lunch. Low-income school districts will have proportionally more kids eligible. PIRLS classified schools into five categories on the basis of the percentage of students in the school eligible for free or reduced-price lunch. The percentage of students eligible and the average reading score in each category were as follows:

Percentage of students eligible	Average reading score
Less than 10%	605
10 to 24.9 percent	584
25 to 49.9 percent	568
50 to 74.9 percent	544
75 percent or more	420

In all cases, students from schools with lower proportions of free lunch eligibility scored higher, on average, than students from schools with higher proportions of free lunch eligibility. These results suggest that the problem is not public schools; it is poverty. Twenty percent of all US schools have poverty rates over 75 percent, and the average ranking of American students reflects this. As repeated studies have shown, the gap in cognitive, physical, and social development between children in poverty and middle-class children is set at an early age. This gap is a result not of billions poured into standardized testing but of the level of poverty in the community.

In regard to the presumed shortage of students in science, technology, engineering, and math (STEM), the reality is complex. In October 2009, *Business Week* reported on a study released by a group of professors at Rutgers and Georgetown academics that found many of the highest-performing students are choosing careers in fields other than STEM. The study suggested that since the late 1990s, many of the top students have been lured away from science and technology to careers in finance and consulting: "Despite decades of complaints that the

United States does not have enough scientists and engineers, the data show our high schools and colleges are providing an ample supply of graduates," said study co-author Hal Salzman, a public policy professor at Rutgers, the State University of New Jersey. "It is now up to science and technology firms to attract the best and the brightest graduates to come work for them."

According to the study, "The top quintile SAT/ACT and GPA performers appear to have been dropping out of the STEM pipeline at a substantial rate, and this decline seems to have come on quite suddenly in the mid-to-late 1990s... The result has been a 'compositional shift to lower-performing students in the STEM pipeline.'"

The decline that Dr. Salzman references happens to have occurred just as Wall Street compensation packages were skyrocketing. The lure of big money was, and still is, hard to resist.

According to *Waiting for Superman*, the education crisis hasn't abated since Sputnik soared overhead in 1957. The poster advertising the film shows a shattered cityscape in dismal tones of gray and black, with a little girl sitting at a desk in the midst of the destruction. As she raises her hand, a beam of light pierces the overhanging clouds and envelops her in a glow of radiance while leaving the surrounding cityscape in darkness. The text reads, "The fate of our country won't be decided on a battlefield. It will be determined in a classroom."

The theme has been seen many times since Sputnik: We are at war with Russia and China, and unless we get our act together, the Sputniks will not only be flying overhead but dropping bombs on our cities.

In addition, it's not an exaggeration to say that the movie poster conveyed a powerful subtext: Rescue your child from her horrible public school! You can almost imagine Davis Guggenheim in his minivan, driving his kids to their private school while watching the neighborhood kids trudge off to the gang wars.

Focus on Teachers

One thing that set *Waiting for Superman* apart from other Sputnik-moment clarion calls was that for the first time an attack was made on educators: Primary targets of *Waiting for Superman* included lazy teachers and the teachers' unions.

The film no doubt tapped into a jealousy that many nonunionized Americans in the workforce feel toward the shrinking segment of the unionized population that enjoys relative job stability, pensions, and health care benefits. This message was superficially appealing as it suggested a clear and manageable solution: break up the teachers' unions and schools would thrive.

Perhaps the writer most associated with the narrative of teachers' unions as villains is Steven Brill. In August 2009 *The New Yorker* published Brill's report on New York City's "rubber rooms," an exposé of the treatment of about forty teachers—one-twentieth of one percent of the district's eighty thousand public school teachers—who had been removed from the classroom because of serious transgressions, such as failing to teach or verbally harassing students. But because these few teachers had been granted tenure by the district, their union contracts entitled them to their full salary until a due process hearing determined whether they would be fired or reassigned. While they awaited hearings, sometimes for as long as three years, they languished in the rubber room. According to Brill, there was no one to blame but the teachers' union.

While this was not a good situation, readers needed to remember that the scenario affected a minuscule number of teachers in a system that employed eighty thousand. And of course unions need to be improved, but it's wise to recall that before teachers unionized, the disparity in pay between men and women was even wider and the arbitrary power of school boards to raise class size or dismiss teachers without any resistance was endemic.

When people cry "*do something*," unions make for a good scapegoat; but, as usual, such efforts are focused on "fixing" schools rather than addressing the underlying social and economic problems that burden our students. In reality, many nations with strong public educational systems have equally strong teacher unions. As *The Nation* reported in September 2010, "In the Finnish education system, which is often cited in the film as the best in the world, teachers are unionized and granted tenure, and families benefit from a cradle-to-grave social welfare system that includes universal daycare, preschool and health care—all of which are proven to help children achieve better results in school."

The film placed opinions of noneducators front and center. Mega-philanthropist Bill Gates, who appears in *Waiting for Superman*, made personal appearances to promote the film; he told an audience at the Toronto International Film Festival that to save money, school districts should cut pension payments for retired teachers.

Newspapers have joined the fray. Ignoring the protests of unions and many education policy experts, the *Los Angeles Times* published a searchable online database of elementary school teachers' effectiveness rankings. The newspaper's rankings were made using a new statistical method called value-added measurement, which was based on children's standardized test scores and which social scientists across the political spectrum agreed was volatile and often flawed.

The film focused on tenure as an impediment to teacher improvement. But even tenured teachers can be fired with due process and for good reason, and surveys suggest that most principals agree they have the authority to fire a teacher if they need to take such action.

Endorsed was the idea that competition for resources is a good thing. Indeed, many people are seduced by the idea that market forces can fix our schools. In reality, as we saw with No Child Left Behind, setting up systems of competition between students, between teachers, and between schools often results in teachers being motivated to assemble only the most promising students, to hide curriculum strategies from peers, and to cheat on standardized tests. Meanwhile, children can become disillusioned by a sink-or-swim atmosphere that threatens them with dire life outcomes if they are not racing to the top of the heap.

In spite of the millions of dollars spent supporting the theory of paying teachers for higher student test scores (sometimes called merit pay), a 2007 study by Vanderbilt University's National Center on Performance Incentives entitled "Project on Incentives in Teaching" (POINT) found that the use of merit pay for teachers in the Nashville school district produced no difference in test outcomes for students.

Everyone would agree that retention of talented teachers is key. A report by the nonprofit National Commission on Teaching and America's Future entitled "The Cost of Teacher Turnover in

Five School Districts" said, "Low performing schools rarely close the student achievement gap because they never close the teaching quality gap—they are constantly rebuilding their staff. An inordinate amount of their capital—both human and financial— is consumed by the constant process of hiring and replacing beginning teachers who leave before they have mastered the ability to create a successful learning culture for their students.

"Student achievement suffers, but high turnover schools are also extremely costly to operate. Trapped in a chronic cycle of teacher hiring and replacement these schools drain their districts of precious dollars that could be better spent to improve teaching quality and student achievement."

Waiting for Superman promoted a bizarre image of learning that asserted that teaching was a matter of pouring information into children's heads. In one of its many little cartoon segments, the film showed the top of a child's head cut open and a jumble of factoids being poured in. Then the bad teachers' union and state regulations stifled this productive pouring process.

With such images, the filmmakers betrayed a lack of understanding of how students actually learn through active and engaged participation in the learning process. They ignored the social acquisition of knowledge and the profound differences between understanding and rote memorization. The audience didn't see what excellent teaching looked like, nor did they learn how often teachers go above and beyond the call of duty to help their students succeed.

An examination of the facts paints a very different picture of American public education than seen in the film. As Valerie Strauss wrote in the *Washington Post*, "Maybe this [analysis] will help persuade those who believed that *Waiting for Superman* unflinchingly showed reality that, in fact, it didn't, and that it is time to take a new look at public education that doesn't demonize teachers and traditional public schools."

Money and Charter Schools

Is a lack of money the problem? The federal government often believes that cash dumped at the door of the schoolhouse is a good solution. In contrast, many conservative commentators think that public schools get *too much* money, and that vouchers should be given to parents to spend on charter or private schools. The answer, we're told by politicians, can be found in independent charter schools that are somehow more "accountable"—although it's not always clear to whom.

In the late twentieth century, charter schools were first proposed by teachers' unions to allow committed parents and teachers to create schools that were free of administrative bureaucracy and open to experimentation and innovation. In 1991, Minnesota wrote the first charter school law in the United States. Since then, some excellent charters have set examples.

But charters are not always islands of integrity and achievement. While teacher unions were vilified in the film, there was no mention of charter corruption, profiteering, or poor performance. And, by their very definition, charter schools are exclusionary. Unlike public schools, which are obligated to accept every eligible student, charter schools can be selective, and based on their charters they can exclude certain students and populations. Thus their performance cannot be accurately measured against public schools.

Even so, the 2013 National Charter School Study by the Center for Research on Education Outcomes at Stanford University

(CREDO) concluded that despite their selective nature, only 17% of charter schools had better test scores than traditional public schools, 46% had gains that were no different than their public counterparts, and 37% were significantly worse.

Ironically, the exclusive charter schools featured in the film receive generous private subsidies. Much of the funding for Geoffrey Canada's Harlem Children's Zone comes from private sources, effectively making his charter school more like a highly resourced private school. There's absolutely nothing wrong with that, but it's not a sustainable model for our nation's public schools. Promise Academy is in many ways an excellent school, but the filmmakers say nothing about the funds it took to create it and the extensive social supports including free medical care and counseling provided by the zone. As *The New York Times* reported on October 12, 2010, "The parent organization of the schools, the Harlem Children's Zone, enjoys substantial largess, much of it from Wall Street. While its cradle-to-college approach, which seeks to break the cycle of poverty for all ten thousand children in a ninety-seven-block zone of Harlem, may be breathtaking in scope, the jury is still out on its overall impact. And the cost of its charter schools—around $16,000 per student in the classroom each year, as well as thousands of dollars in out-of-class spending—has raised questions about their utility as a nationwide model."

The Children's Zone's charter schools are open to all city children by lottery. According to *The New York Times*, each year the schools spend, per student, $12,443 in public money and $3,482 in private financing. But that does not include the costs of the after-school program, rewards for student performance, a chef who prepares healthy meals, central administration and most building costs, and some of the expense of the students' free health and dental care, which come out of the zone's overall budget, not the school's budget.

While the nation's public education problems are more systemic than the resources of any given school, and money will not solve all problems, ignoring the discussion of resources is problematic. The use of charters as a sledgehammer by those who would outsource and privatize education in the name of "reform" is highly misguided.

In *Waiting for Superman*, the filmmakers depicted the raw emotions of families as they waited in an auditorium for an admission lottery where the winners' names are pulled from a hat and read aloud. The losing families left in tears with cameras shoved in their faces. It is not a sustainable public policy to divert more and more public school funding to privately subsidized charters while public schools become the destinations of last resort for children with the greatest educational needs.

Standardized Testing

How do you measure success in school? The film fell back on the standard metric of using test scores as an indication of success. Under this system, higher test scores means better school performance and more highly educated students. But the debate of *how* to raise test scores invariably distorts the task of identifying and solving our education challenges. If the problem has been defined as low test scores, then the framers of the argument leave little possibility that there could be other problem possibilities. With that in mind, there is always a move to *do something* to fix the teachers, fix the students, and fix the failing schools. Defining the problem as low test scores implies that the problem is one dimensional and it also implies that if the teachers, students, and schools only worked harder, longer, and did more, somehow test scores would improve.

Test scores are not the *problem* but a *symptom*. I submit that low test scores are an outcome of a much more intense set of problems that have yet to be addressed.

As Abraham Maslow revealed, humans have a hierarchy of needs. These needs must be satisfied in order. Based on Maslow's theory, a human being cannot satisfy the higher needs without first satisfying the lower needs of food, shelter, and safety—not to mention esteem. A child whose basic needs are not being met will have a much more difficult time becoming engaged in school and, ultimately, performing well on tests.

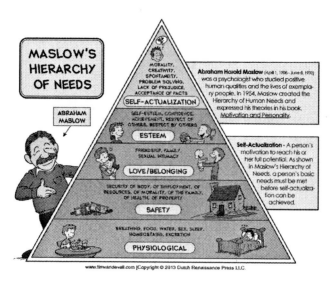

When schools focus exclusively on boosting scores on standardized tests, they dumb down the curriculum, reduce teachers to function as test-prep robots, ignore important subject areas and critical thinking skills, and leave children less prepared for the future. We need a deeper and authentic assessment to understand if schools are doing poorly and, if so, how to help them improve.

Sadly, schools and teachers continue to take the blame for huge social inequities in housing, health care, and income. Poverty is an issue that remains at the very center of the challenge. Between 1970 and today, income disparities between the richest and poorest in US society have reached record levels. Poor communities continue to suffer extensive dislocations and traumas. The exploitation of immigrants, homelessness, lack of meaningful jobs, and the closing of community health and counseling clinics are all factors that shape our school communities. "Do-something" solutions and sugar pills that cosmetically dress up schools without addressing the underlying conditions only increase the marginalization of poor children.

Charter schools and the increasing privatization of public education are not the answers. The large corporations promote the idea that public education is "failing" and students deserve "choices." But this is no solution; it's merely another way to *do something*. The fix never seems to work because it does not address the root problems. When mom and dad have no jobs, when they're in danger of losing their home, when there is no proper medical care, when kids are hungry, when the home is in the line of fire, it doesn't take a rocket scientist to figure out that it is difficult for children to do well in school.

The Every Student Succeeds Act

In late 2015, the impulse to do something entered a new phase with the passage of the federal Every Student Succeeds Act. The bill, sponsored by Senators Lamar Alexander (R-Tenn.) and Patty Murray (D-Wash.), and Representatives John Kline (R-Minn.) and Bobby Scott (D-Va.), was seen as the final replacement for the much-despised No Child Left Behind Act of 2001. For the first time in nearly a quarter century, ESSA would roll back the federal presence in K-12 education, giving states more control in the areas of accountability, teacher evaluation, school turnarounds, and more.

The bipartisan bill passed by the House includes many of the key reforms the Administration has called on Congress to enact and encouraged states and districts to adopt in exchange for waivers offering relief from the more onerous provisions of No Child Left Behind.

- Holding all students to high standards that prepare them for success in college and careers
- Ensuring accountability by guaranteeing that when students fall behind, states redirect resources into what works to help them and their schools improve, with a particular focus on the way lowest-performing schools, high schools with high dropout rates, and schools with achievement gaps.
- Empowering state and local decision-makers to develop their own strong systems for school improvement based upon evidence, rather than imposing cookie-cutter federal solutions like the No Child Left Behind Act did.

- Reducing the often onerous burden of testing on students and teachers, making sure that tests don't crowd out teaching and learning, without sacrificing clear, annual information parents and educators need to make sure our children are learning.
- Providing more children access to high quality preschool.
- Establishing new resources for proven strategies that will spur reform and drive opportunity and better outcomes for America's students.

As they had so many times before, politicians on both sides of the aisle were quick to congratulate each other on the passage of yet another federal education bill. Cosmetically, there were some changes from previous efforts. Under ESSA, which was the newest version of the 1965 Elementary and Secondary Education Act, states would get to decide whether to stay with teacher evaluations through student outcomes (in place in forty-two states and the District of Columbia) and the Common Core standards in place in more than forty states. And while ESSA would maintain annual tests, states could reduce the role those assessments played in school ratings and accountability, giving more weight to other factors such as like school climate, teacher engagement, and access to advanced coursework.

"It is the single biggest step toward local control of public schools in twenty-five years," said Senator Alexander, chair of the Senate education panel. Alexander said it would "unleash a flood of innovation and student achievement across America, community by community and state by state."

The measure also sought to maintain what Murray and Scott called important "guardrails" to fix struggling schools and help close the achievement gap between groups of students facing challenges—those in poverty, racial minorities, students in special education, and English-language learners—and their peers.

Another major provision of ESSA was that it sought to streamline the US Department of Education, consolidating nearly fifty programs into a single block grant, and aimed to curb the authority of the US secretary of education in the areas of standards, assessments, school turnarounds, teacher evaluation, and others.

The language restricting the power of the secretary of education was largely seen as a response to President Obama's secretary of education Arne Duncan, who, conservatives complained, had overstepped the bounds of his office in issuing conditional waivers and granting flexibility from NCLB in exchange for certain policy promises.

Despite the usual enthusiasm with which the bill was greeted, many policy analysts saw considerable ambiguity and many unanswered questions.

"The bill leaves a lot of gray, murky areas and uses some words that are open to interpretation," said Chad Aldeman, an associate partner at Bellwether Education Partners. "Depending on what the secretary [of education] tries to do, I think it could open him up to lawsuits."

For example, ESSA called for states and districts to identify, and help fix, schools where traditionally overlooked groups of students were "consistently underperforming." But what, exactly, did that phrase mean? And did states get to define it, or did the US Department of Education?

On December 7, 2015 The Washington Post published an article by Valerie Strauss entitled "The successor to No Child Left Behind has, it turns out, big problems of its own." Among the concerns she cited were:

- Use of federal funds for "Pay for Success" programs allowed wealthy investors to make profits from education investments, an issue that had concerned some special education advocates.
- States would be required to fund "equitable services" for children in private and religious schools who are deemed eligible, and they must appoint an "ombudsman" to make sure the schools get their money.
- Provisions in the legislation for the establishment of teacher preparation academies were written to primarily support non-traditional, non-university programs such as those funded by venture philanthropists, and they lowered standards for teacher education programs that prepared teachers for high-poverty schools.
- The federal government would still have influence certain areas such as mandating standardized tests and requiring states to intercede in schools where student test scores are in the lowest five percent and then approving the state plans for academic progress.

Since ESSA wouldn't be fully in place until the 2017-18 school year, the heavy lifting of monitoring and implementation would fall on the shoulders of the following administration.

The bottom line, of course, is that ESSA was nothing more than old wine in a new bottle. The core concept was identical to what had been tried over and over again by the federal government since the days of Sputnik: Pour federal dollars into the schools while doing nothing for the students who walked through the doors and the communities in which they lived.

You can't get a summer job? Not our problem—but you'd better ace the test we're going to give you.

Your mom is working for poverty wages at a fast-food restaurant? Can't help you there—but you'd better show the required academic progress.

There are gangs outside the schoolyard? Call the cops.

You have to ride two buses for an hour to get to school? Hey, Abe Lincoln used to walk to school, so don't complain.

Don't speak much English? You'd better start studying!

And, dear student, if you can't succeed at the local public school, it means that either 1) Public schools are inherently bad, and you should try to get into a charter school, or 2) You're caught in the "cycle of poverty" and it's your fault you can't get out.

It would not take a crystal ball to predict that ESSA, like all the other "fix-the-schools" programs before it that had ended at the fence around the schoolyard, wouldn't produce results that were any different from its predecessors.

The Urge to Do
What's Politically Expedient

Everyone wants the United States to have terrific schools that graduate bright, capable students.

And when a perceived crisis looms—whether it's a Soviet satellite, a book, or a movie—the popular response is to take action to "fix" our schools.

In discussing the perceived problem of our nation's schools, policymakers in Washington manage to agree on a basic set of facts: The Constitution of the United States makes no mention of education, thereby leaving it a matter entirely to the states. Our nation's schools are decentralized, reflect their local communities, and vary widely in their characteristics, from the makeup of the student body to the expectations of administrators and teachers.

That's where the agreement ends.

Some policymakers think that the decentralized, local approach is a good thing, and is both in keeping with the intent of the Constitution and a reasonable education model. Others believe that a modern industrialized nation like the United States should have greater uniformity of education, so that a high school diploma means the same thing regardless of the school that awarded it.

Some believe that the states must have educational sovereignty. Others believe that state sovereignty is an approach better left where it began, in the eighteenth century.

It's difficult to reach a consensus in Washington. When it comes to doing something about education, since the time of Sputnik the various political factions have historically been able to agree on one course of action and one goal: to raise student test scores.

Politicians on both sides of the aisle agree: Get those test scores up! Higher test scores will prove that we're doing better!

The question then becomes, "How do you raise test scores?"

The follow-up questions are, "Who should write the tests? What constitutes the 'right' answer that signifies a student has learned something? Should the 'right' answer be the same in every school across America?"

For many, the answer is standards-based education, in which students are expected to know an agreed-upon set of facts and possess a standard set of skills based on their grade level.

For example—and this is an extremely simple, hypothetical case—let's say the English standard for first grade is this: Every student must be able to read and understand the sentence, "Sally walked up the hill to find her dog." If a student can read that sentence, he or she passes. If not, he or she does not pass. Other factors don't matter. If the student didn't have breakfast, if the student is a non-English speaker, if the student has a volatile home situation—these environmental conditions don't matter. Only the fact of acquiring stated knowledge and skills matters.

There's a flip side to this scenario as well. What if the student is advanced relative to his or her grade level, and can easily pass the test and is capable of handling bigger challenges?

The standards-based approach fails such a student just as surely as it fails students who, for whatever reason, aren't as capable. When you aim to funnel all students into a single norm, you do a disservice to two groups: the students who are below the norm and those who are above it. In American classroom education, this standards-based approach didn't exist until the end of the twentieth century. Individual school districts in individual states traditionally enjoyed the freedom to create their own curricula and measure student progress as they chose.

In fact, it may be useful to turn back the clock to the days of the rural one-room schoolhouse. In such a community school, every school-age child—say, from age five to fifteen—would report to the school, where there was one teacher. Let's say that our Prairie School had twenty students—the size of an average class today. In such a situation, it would be difficult, if not ludicrous, to attempt to teach to the test because you'd have one teacher administering twenty different tests to twenty different students of varying academic levels. Instead, what was required was for the teacher to *meet* each child at his or her level and work from there.

To one student the teacher would say, "Hi, Sally. You're eight years old. Can you read this McGuffey Reader? Yes? How about this more advanced reader? Do you want to try it? All right, you can try the advanced reader."

Then to the next student the teacher would say, "Hi, Johnny. You're seven years old. Can you read this McGuffey Reader? No? All right, here's one that's a little bit easier."

In fact, in the Prairie School it was routine for older kids to be put into service tutoring the younger kids. This provided each child with even more personalized attention.

Did such a system work? It certainly did for many; presidents Abraham Lincoln and Herbert Hoover were both educated in one-room schools; and young Henry Ford attended the one-room Miller School and then the Scotch Settlement School in Dearborn, Michigan.

The point is that in a one-room schoolhouse, teaching is an *organic* endeavor exemplified by a personal relationship between teacher and student, in which the teacher meets the student at his or her level and works from there.

Today, we see increasing focus on standards-based education, which demands that the students rise (or even *lower* themselves!) to the level set by a school administrator or education consultant. Proponents argue that this approach makes our children better prepared for college and the job market.

Here's where it can get tricky. Not only do politicians want to measure the achievement of our students against a standard test, but they also want to know how effective the *schools* are. They want to use tests not only to measure the achievement of the students but also of the school's ability to move the students through the grades. Politicians ask, "If we appropriate billions for better schools, we need to be able to measure that the taxpayer's money makes a difference." They want to know not only individual student *achievement* but the overall *progress* of all the students in a school.

This raises another thorny issue. Can we expect all schools to show the same rate of progress for their students? Should the school in the low-income neighborhood, or the neighborhood with a high percentage of non-English-speaking students, be expected to work miracles and show that its students are making the same progress as classroom-ready students in wealthy districts?

For many students, learning English and mastering basic math represent two real achievements. For other students, advanced work in English literature and calculus might represent an equivalent amount of effort and progress. Progress and achievement are very different metrics, and they are in a constant state of tension. Proponents of a strictly standards-based education advocate for determining student and/ or school success by measuring only achievement as opposed to also measuring progress. Other educators believe that if you only measure achievement—a test score—you're missing not only how far a student may have risen, but also a wide range of other skills and attributes that are equally necessary for a well-rounded, productive citizen to have.

Can a test score measure the ability to collaborate? Or assess creativity? Or reveal leadership skills? Or evaluate personal tenacity? For success in life, these and many other personal attributes come into play.

We're not talking about handing out gratuitous trophies for "effort" and "participation"—gestures that many people think dilute legitimate achievement. We're talking about the real world and the characteristics of people who become not only productive citizens but leaders. By what standard should they be measured in school? And who should do the measuring?

Educators have been grappling with this question ever since Plato wondered if his students, whom he taught while sitting under the tree, were really listening to him or just nodding their heads while they daydreamed.

Assuming for a moment that the acceptance of standards has been agreed upon, then further questions that educators grapple with are: *What* are the standards, and *how* do you teach your students to meet those standards?

According to the Glossary of Education Reform, the term "standards-based" refers to systems of instruction, assessment, grading, and academic reporting that are based on students demonstrating an understanding or mastery of the knowledge and skills they are expected to learn as they progress through their education. In a school that uses standards-based approaches to educating students, learning standards—i.e., concise, written descriptions of what students are expected to know and be able to do at a specific stage of their education—determine the goals of a lesson or course, and teachers then determine how and what to teach students so they achieve the learning expectations described in the standards.

In other words, you "teach to the test."

It's a method that has its attributes. It's like the first-grade teacher who says, "Johnny, can you tell me what two plus two equals? Your answer is 'four'? Good. You pass the test."

If 2+2=4 weren't part of the standard for first grade—if it weren't on the test—then the teacher probably wouldn't waste the taxpayers' money teaching it. She'd stick to the standard.

Standards-based education is said to focus on the *outcome*—the test score. It refers to the practice of determining, through tests or some other means, that students have learned what they were taught and have achieved the expected standards. Teachers work to ensure that students can demonstrate that they've learned the expected material as they progress in their education. When the first-grade teacher asks Johnny to add two plus two, the answer is the standard: four.

In the United States, even with Common Core, most standards-based approaches to educating students use state learning standards to determine academic expectations and define "proficiency" in a given course, subject area, or grade level. Standards-based learning is common in American elementary schools, but it is becoming more widely used in middle and secondary schools. Who, then, sets the standards? And how *achievable* are they? The second question is very important.

For example, just about anyone will agree that a first-grader should know that two plus two equals four. It's a simple standard. But the human impulse—and especially the *government* impulse—is to make things complicated. The old saying "less is more" is often good advice, but the political reality is that greater complexity makes a program or initiative more appealing to a wide sample of stakeholders who may have conflicting ideas.

Most teachers will tell you that students learn more when they're taught less but taught well. Unfortunately, this principle is too often violated in the standards documents. Because it's easier to add and enlarge than to reduce and refine, we have often failed to place hard but practical limits on the number and the nature of the standards. The result (perhaps for political reasons) has been far too many demands for inclusion in the standards documents, creating complex and poorly written standards that almost no one can realistically teach to or ever hope to adequately assess.

In the case of standards, quantity is not quality. For example, as Mike Schmoker and Robert J. Marzano wrote in *Educational Leadership*, the Third International Mathematics and Science Study (TIMSS) revealed that although US mathematics textbooks attempt to cover 175 percent more topics than do German textbooks and 350 percent more topics than do Japanese textbooks, both German and Japanese students significantly outperform US students in mathematics tests. Similarly, while

US science textbooks address 930 percent more topics than do German textbooks and 433 percent more topics than do Japanese textbooks, both German and Japanese students significantly outperform US students in science achievement.

While the concept of minimum standards is logical, the impulse is toward complexity, and schools might benefit from decreasing the amount of content they're required to cover. Teacher morale and self-efficacy improve when schools clearly describe a manageable number of essential topics to be taught and assessed in greater depth.

The Politics of Education

Aside from the rush to *do something* during a time of perceived education crisis, efforts to "fix" schools are inevitably shaped by politics.

What we see over and over again in the politics of education in America is the tension between the federal government and the states, and the impulse to craft initiatives that are acceptable to both. The states want autonomy but they also want federal dollars. The federal government, and in particular the executive branch, wants national standards for education, while individual legislators—who come from the states, after all—want to steer federal dollars into their communities in a manner that's acceptable to conservative voters.

When the cry arises to *do something*, the result is a hastily prepared program involving the distribution of federal money to the states. Regardless of the program, federal funds are awarded according to a delicately balanced and complex structure that carefully avoids any federal meddling in *communities* (where the students come from) and instead seeks to improve *schools* (where students arrive every morning).

As more than one observer has noted, such an approach serves to romanticize the low-income student, an impulse which conforms to the conservative view of American society. According to this view, every student who walks through the schoolhouse door has the same capability for achievement as every other. The student from a broken home has the same capability for success as the student from a stable home. The student who lives in a slum has the same capability for success as the student who lives in a comfortable suburb.

But if we return to Maslow's hierarchy of needs, it's easy to see how this simply isn't possible. A student whose basic needs of food, shelter, and security are not being met will have a much more difficult time addressing additional challenges, and is much more likely to view school work as either irrelevant or an onerous burden.

It's easy for grownups to say, "All kids should perform to the standard!" To give the problem a different perspective, imagine two adults working at the same office job. "Joe" has a secure home, drives his own car to work, owns the appropriate workplace clothing, and is signed up for health care. "George," meanwhile, lives in a slum, must take two buses to work, owns old clothes, and has no health insurance. Who among us would expect that George's job performance would match Joe's? In fact, don't we lavish luxuries on valued employees like Joe so that they can "focus on the job" more effectively and not have to worry about managing their private lives? High-performing executives are provided with chauffeured cars, expense account lunches, and dry cleaning services. The rationale is that by freeing them of everyday burdens, they'll excel at their corporate jobs. No one wants the CEO of a Fortune 500 company to stand on the street corner in the rain, waiting for the bus to take him to work. If he were forced to do that, we'd assume his job performance would suffer. This approach underlines Maslow's theory: when the basic needs of a human being are provided for, the person is able to achieve more. If it's accepted as dogma in the business world, why not in school?

Proponents of standards-based education are quick to point out "the exceptional George": The person who overcame poverty and disadvantage to rise through the ranks to go to college and become a leader in business or politics. They say, "Look at so-and-so. He was born in a ghetto and now he's a rich man. If he can do it, then anyone can!" The evening news programs offer no shortage of politicians who assert that since they pulled themselves up by their bootstraps and walked five miles to school every day, any kid in America should be able to do the same thing.

Yes, there are exceptional people who defy the odds and manage to succeed despite tremendous adversity. They are inspiring cases. But that's no justification for expecting every child to be able to do the same. The exceptional student only proves that students are diverse and highly individualized. In the aggregate—across a wide sample of children—there can be no doubt that when basic social and economic needs are unmet, students have much greater difficulty in school.

Many proponents of school funding promote the theory that if we were to provide the *same school* for every student, then there would be no reason why the outcomes would not be the same at each school.

The theory is that each and every school should be capable of taking every student up to the standard. If the school cannot do this, then there must be a problem with the *school*: the teachers' union is too powerful, there aren't enough computers for the kids, the teachers haven't been trained properly, the curriculum is wrong, the parents don't care enough about their kids' educations.

Politicians say that the way to fix these problems is to give the school—and the education industry as a whole—more money to spend.

Even this simplistic approach can run into resistance. And every politician has his or her own fervently held beliefs and favorite education villains.

In August 2015, Governor Chris Christie, who was running for president of the United States, said that the academic achievement gap couldn't be fixed until after a "fundamental fight" with the teachers unions.

"We know how to fix this, but we're not doing it," he said during an interview with Campbell Brown, of the Partnership for Educational Justice and the74million.org, at an education summit in New Hampshire. "We're not doing it because the teachers' unions and the educational establishment, not only in New Jersey but across the country, know that the necessary fixes will take apart the monopoly they have on education... And until we have that fundamental fight in this country as to who's going to run education in this country, parents or unions, until we fix that and come to a conclusion on that, we're not going to be able to fix the achievement gap." He later said that schools without teachers unions would be "nirvana."

Common Core, which to many represents a nationalized curriculum, has been attacked by both the right and, perhaps surprisingly, the left. As *U.S. News & World Report* reported, on the right, school-choice voucher proponents, along with home-schooling advocates, conservative Christian academies, and parochial-education groups, have used the fight over Common Core to help them recruit disgruntled parents and spearhead the fight to abolish the federal Department of Education.

Freedom Works, a conservative group, has produced anti–Common Core videos as well as a political action plan, and has publicly stated it will mobilize supporters to pressure local officials to promote private school vouchers and work against teacher unions and tenure.

Conservative broadcaster Glenn Beck has asserted that Common Core is a backdoor means for the government to spy on citizens and indoctrinate children in what Beck called "an extreme liberal ideology."

Meanwhile, critics on the left see a rigid, one-size-fits-all approach, drafted by politicians in back rooms, that ignores how teachers teach and how children learn. They fear the curriculum, and the standardized testing, only amplifies the high-pressure, high-stakes atmosphere that No Child Left Behind helped create.

Teachers often approve of the concept of Common Core but dislike its implementation. They complain the curriculum, created without teacher input, is too rigid, its dissemination was haphazard, and administrators and parents will blame them if student test scores plummet. Common Core backers didn't seek participation from teachers, who believe that rushing from one high-stakes test to another is the wrong approach.

For example, in February 2014 the National Education Association (NEA), which initially embraced Common Core, criticized the "completely botched" rollout. In a letter to the union's three million members, NEA President Dennis Van Roekel declared the standards would fail without more input from teachers and a "major course correction."

Opponents on the left also assert that the multibillion-dollar educational testing industry and corporate textbook manufacturers like McGraw-Hill are major beneficiaries of Common Core. They are deeply suspicious of the support for Common Core by groups including the Business Roundtable and the US Chamber of Commerce; they think that such groups want to produce robotic workers while profiting from the sale of education materials and software.

The disputes erupted within the states themselves. A bitter fight over the future of academic standards in Louisiana generated dueling lawsuits between Governor Bobby Jindal and the state superintendent of education he had appointed. A group of parents and teachers and a charter school operator went to court in Baton Rouge to argue that the governor's withdrawal of the state from a testing contract aligned with the Common Core amounted to an "attempt to usurp the authority" of the legislature and the board of education. Jindal, a Republican who had presidential aspirations for 2016, had become an outspoken detractor of academic standards that he ardently supported when the state originally adopted them in 2010. Many conservatives regarded opposition to the Common Core as a litmus test; Governor Jindal's critics said he changed his views mainly to court Tea Party supporters.

In the US Congress, the debate continues. In July 2015, the US House passed a Republican rewrite of the No Child Left Behind education law, with party leaders seeking to gain support from conservative members who balked earlier that year.

The House bill, HR 5, also called the Student Success Act, was intended to cut back the federal government's role in K–12 education and would eliminate dozens of programs that Republicans say are duplicative.

One proposed amendment, sponsored by Representatives Matt Salmon of Arizona and Ron DeSantis of Florida, would ease federal testing mandates. "This will effectively release the federal testing mandate on students, with no penalties to schools," said Representative Salmon.

Another amendment, proposed by Representative Mark Walker of North Carolina and DeSantis, would let states opt out of federal education programs without giving up some funding, and allow them to consolidate some federal funding for other education purposes.

The amendment "frees states of this top-down, one-size-all approach to education and empowers the community to determine how to best use federal funding," Walker said.

"Every child deserves the opportunity to attend a great school, pursue their dreams, and achieve the American dream," said spokesman Kevin Smith. "That's what the Student Success Act is all about, and the speaker is proud to support this legislation."

The "Student Success Bill Fact Sheet" released in February 2015 by the Congressional Education and the Workforce Committee, chaired by US Representative John Kline (R-MN), sounded a familiar refrain, including the oft-repeated assertion that in America, "the K–12 education system is broken." The report claimed:

Every child in every school deserves access to an excellent education. Unfortunately, the country continues to fall far short of reaching that goal. The federal government's involvement in local K–12 schools is at an all-time high, yet student achievement remains stagnant. Approximately one out of every five students drops out of high school. Many that do graduate lack the knowledge and skills necessary to pursue a postsecondary education and compete in the workforce. Only 38 percent of high school seniors can read at grade level, and 26 percent are proficient in math. The K–12 education system is broken, making it harder for countless children to enjoy a life of opportunity and success.

Although No Child Left Behind was based on good intentions, there is broad, bipartisan agreement the law needs to be replaced. Even the president agrees, yet he has been unwilling to work with Congress to change the law. Instead, the administration has created a convoluted waiver process that replaces some of the law's more onerous requirements with new mandates dictated by the Secretary of Education—compounding the confusion and frustration shared by states and schools.

THE SOLUTION: It is time to reform a flawed law and improve K–12 education. Congress must replace No Child Left Behind with new policies that help every child access an excellent education. Toward that end, House Education and the Workforce Committee Chairman John Kline (R-MN) and Early Childhood,

Elementary, and Secondary Education Subcommittee Chairman Todd Rokita (R-IN) have introduced the Student Success Act (HR 5). The legislation will reduce the federal footprint, restore local control, and empower parents and education leaders to hold schools accountable for effectively teaching students. HR 5 – STUDENT SUCCESS ACT: Replaces the current national accountability scheme based on high stakes tests with state-led accountability systems, returning responsibility for measuring student and school performance to states and school districts.

- Ensures parents continue to have the information they need to hold local schools accountable.
- Eliminates more than 65 ineffective, duplicative, and unnecessary programs and replaces this maze of programs with a Local Academic Flexible Grant, helping schools better support students.
- Protects state and local autonomy over decisions in the classroom by preventing the Secretary of Education from coercing states into adopting Common Core or any other common standards or assessments, as well as reining in the secretary's regulatory authority.
- Empowers parents with more school choice options by continuing support for magnet schools and expanding charter school opportunities, as well as allowing Title I funds to follow low-income children to the traditional public or charter school of the parent's choice.

- Strengthens existing efforts to improve student performance among targeted student populations, including English learners and homeless children.

The message in the "Student Success Bill Fact Sheet" was clear: *Our schools are broken because of too much federal intervention.* We should just give the money to the states and let them spend it as they wish. We should also give low-income families more educational "choices."

The idea of giving low-income families the "choice" to send their kids across town to a charter school or private school has perennial appeal to conservative lawmakers. It places "the family" front and center, and takes the burden of improving our neighborhoods off the back of the taxpayers.

In reality, making such choices possible would involve the direct intervention into the fabric of poor neighborhoods: jobs programs, infrastructure projects, community resources.

The Senate considered its own version of the education bill, which would give states authority to determine how to hold school districts accountable for student performance.

"The needs of a student in eastern Kentucky aren't likely to be the same as those of students in south Florida or downtown Manhattan," Senate Majority Leader Mitch McConnell of Kentucky said on the Senate floor. "This bill would give states the flexibility to develop systems that work for the needs of their students, rather than the one-size-fits-all mandate of Washington."

Meanwhile, on the left, second-ranking House Democrat Steny Hoyer of Maryland said that his party "will overwhelmingly oppose this bill... When Republicans can't get agreement on a bill, they move further to the right. They don't move toward consensus. They move toward greater confrontation."

The White House budget office issued a statement urging revisions to the Senate measure to "strengthen school accountability to close troubling achievement and opportunity gaps, including by requiring interventions and supports" in low-performing schools. "Parents, families, and communities deserve to know that when children fall behind, their schools will take action to improve," said the administration's statement.

The reality is that students from low-income families comprise a big chunk of the US public school population. Many of our nation's children live in conditions of perpetual poverty, with few educational resources in their homes or communities. Their parents face food insecurity, unemployment, a lack of safe and affordable housing, and many other challenges that diminish their children's opportunities to learn. Clean, safe schools with substantial resources can make an important difference in the lives of children, but schools cannot serve as the nation's primary antipoverty program. The presumed cause and effect is too tenuous and, as we have learned too painfully, prescribing sugar pills in the form of cash to schools does not address the significant underlying problems.

What Has Testing Accomplished?

Even as No Child Left Behind has fallen further and further into disrepute, the idea of standardized testing lingers. But many experts assert that such testing—the central idea of NCLB—hasn't shown much usefulness.

As Kevin Welner and William Mathis wrote in "Reauthorization of the Elementary and Secondary Education Act: Time to Move

Beyond Test-Focused Policies" for the National Education Policy Center, "Since NCLB became law in 2002, students may have shown slight increases in test scores, relative to pre-NCLB students. Looking at the results of the National Assessment of Educational Progress (NAEP), however, any test score increases over the pre-NCLB trend are very small, and they are miniscule compared to what early advocates of NCLB promised. We as a nation have devoted enormous amounts of time and money to the focused goal of increasing test scores, and we have almost nothing to show for it. Just as importantly, there is no evidence that any test score increases represent the broader learning increases that were the true goals of the policy—goals such as critical thinking; the creation of lifelong learners; and more students graduating high school ready for college, career, and civic participation. While testing advocates proclaim that testing drives student learning, they resist evidence-based explanations for why, after two decades of test-driven accountability, these reforms have yielded such unimpressive results."

The formula seemed so simple:

1. Pour billions of dollars into our schools.
2. The billions will help us educate our children better.
3. We'll see the results with improved test scores.

Somehow, the formula hasn't worked.

What Do Parents Want?

Too often, left out of the debate is what parents want and how they feel about the schools in their communities.

One highly respected and widely followed source for such information is the Phi Delta Kappa/Gallup poll. The annual poll is a scientifically based survey of more than one thousand Americans eighteen years and older. The report of the poll, which is available to anyone online, publishes all questions exactly as they were asked during telephone polling, which most recently occurred in May–June 2015. The PDK/Gallup poll found that most respondents thought highly of their local public schools but not of American public school education in general. Perhaps this is not surprising in light of the endless well-funded campaigns such as *Waiting for Superman* that seek to destroy confidence in American public education. Since the days of Sputnik, the public has heard the endless drumbeat that our public schools are failing, declining, and broken, yet somehow our nation continues to lead the world by most measures of productivity and economic growth, scientific discovery, and technological innovation. Impartial test results such as those found by PIRLS reveal that in general our public schools perform well—it's the schools in *neighborhoods of poverty* that fall behind.

The PDK/Gallup poll revealed that the public is fed up with the emphasis on standardized testing in their local public schools. Nearly half the public supports opting out of mandated standardized tests. Fifty-four percent don't want their public schools to implement the Common Core standards. As the PDK/Gallup press release stated, "A strong majority (about eight in ten) of Americans believe how engaged students are with their classwork and their level of hope for the future are very important for measuring the effectiveness of the public schools in their community. Fewer rated the percentage of graduates attending college and getting a job right after high school as very important. Testing came in last as a measure of effectiveness with just 14% of public school parents rating test scores as very important, making it the last in the list of options."

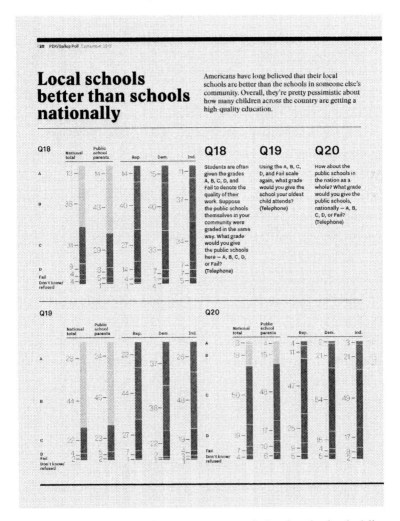

The public "strongly opposes any federal role in holding public schools accountable." This negative feeling is no doubt a reaction to years of No Child Left Behind testing plus additional years of Race to the Top, both of which have produced few tangible benefits but plenty of parent, student, and teacher stress. Fifty-five percent of the public opposes the use of student test scores to evaluate teachers; among public school parents this rises to 63 percent.

While the idea of school choice (among public schools) is attractive to a majority, only 31% of Americans favor allowing students and parents to choose a private school to attend at public expense, a concept commonly known as vouchers. The fact is that Americans tend to like the school that's in their neighborhood; as PDK/Gallup said, "Americans consistently give the highest grades to the schools that are closest to them and that they may have more experience with and the lowest grades to the schools farthest away, a pattern that has held across forty years of the PDK/Gallup poll."

Most American parents—even those in areas of poverty—aren't interested in shipping their child across town to a different school that may be "better" than the school in their neighborhood. What they want is for their *neighborhood* to be better—more jobs, more safety, more opportunity. When you elevate the community, the school rises with it.

What History Tells Us

Albert Einstein said that insanity can be defined as doing the same thing over and over again while expecting a different result. Anyone who has either studied or experienced firsthand the attempts at education reform that have been undertaken on a regular basis in the United States must agree that we are caught in a dismal cycle. Since people first demanded that educators "do something" as Sputnik glided overhead until today, the pattern of alarm followed by activism has been repeated.

The cycle is always the same.

First comes a trigger—a foreign power launches a satellite, a scholarly report is published, a movie is made.

The trigger provokes a wave of fear and questioning. Are we falling behind? Can we meet the challenges of the future? Are our kids doomed to flip burgers for the rest of their lives?

Without fail, the facile answer is the same: We have a national problem. Our kids aren't getting the education they need. The kids in China or Russia or Japan are getting a better education and will outperform our kids in the world marketplace.

Having announced that we *have* a problem—a conclusion drawn with no real attempt to rationally measure what our students actually achieve in the real world, where it counts—the next step is a race to identify the *cause* of the problem.

The cause of the perceived problem is always the schools, and in particular the *public* schools. (Reformers tend to assume our private schools are uniformly excellent, and therefore exempt from scrutiny.)

The public schools, they say, fail to produce the caliber of graduates that our nation needs to be competitive. This failure is rooted in the various component parts of every individual school. These component parts include curricula, teachers, textbooks, testing programs, school lunch programs—all the things that together make up both individual schools and the education industry.

Therefore, the logic goes, if we do three things to improve our schools—and the component parts within them—we will solve our problem and America will remain on top.

These three solutions, which traditionally have been politically agreeable to both liberals and conservatives, are:

1. Give more federal money to schools, school districts, and states.
2. Raise education standards so that our kids will have better skills than kids in other countries.
3. Measure the outcomes by testing. Reward the schools that succeed and punish those that fall behind.

In one variation or another, this is what we've been doing for the past sixty years. And yet the cycle continues. All that it takes to launch the next cycle is a new trigger.

Meanwhile the fundamental questions go unanswered.

Is there really a disease?

If so, is it universal, or does it affect only a portion of our public schools?

What's the cause or causes?

If we have identified the cause, then how do we treat it?

In our choice of treatment, are we really treating the disease? Or are we merely dispensing expensive placebos?

It's time that we take a big step back and reassess both the rationale for our efforts at education reform during the past sixty years and the results we've obtained. We need to question every step of the cycle and not take anything for granted. We need to let go of our preconceptions and look at our system of education with fresh, unbiased eyes.

In doing this, we need to accept that not all schools are created equal. From Key West to the North Slope of Alaska, from coastal Maine to Honolulu, our nation's schools reflect the rich diversity of our neighborhoods.

Likewise, not all students are identical. Our students come to their schools with a wide range of abilities, interests, and expectations.

We also need to accept that over the past sixty years, our "one-size-fits-all" approach to education reform has not made the difference that we expected.

Having learned from the past, we can agree that a fresh approach without preconceptions might look something like this.

1. We must first determine if there is a problem that needs to be fixed. We can't begin to do this until we first agree on how we measure success (or lack thereof). For example, to measure the success of our schools, should we compare our tenth-graders' test scores in math with

those of tenth-grade students in Finland? Or should we compare how many patents are issued each year to graduates of US high schools as compared to foreign high school graduates? This is not a frivolous question; we can recall that the original Sputnik moment resulted in the widespread conviction that American students were falling behind in science and math when compared to their counterparts in the Soviet Union. In reality, they weren't behind—our space program was just on a different schedule. If we believe that our schools are "failing," the imperative question must be, "Compared to what?"

2. If a problem is perceived, it must be defined effectively. This takes detached objectivity, free of preconceptions. The problem(s) that we identify might take the form of a collection of loosely related problems rather than one big problem. For example, a school that appears to be underperforming may be facing a bundle of unrelated problems such as kids who arrive at school hungry, disengaged parents, poorly paid teachers, lack of safe playgrounds—the list could go on.
Experience tells us that to improve the education process in low-performing schools today, we cannot simply say, "We're going to change your curriculum and raise the standards." Schools are organic parts of the communities that they serve, and our efforts to identify and solve problems must take into account the social and economic context in which the students—and their families—live.

3. Given our experience over the past sixty years, it's safe to say that there is no "one size fits all" solution. There are roughly 98,000 public schools in the United States. They are located in rich neighborhoods and poor ones, in cities and in rural areas, in places where everyone speaks English and places where many students speak another language at home. While the federal government may have the best of intentions when it creates its vast education reform programs, it cannot possibly provide the kind of granular support that is needed to affect not just individual schools but individual classrooms and even individual students. Given the tremendous diversity of our schools, in every situation there may not be a single best practice. Any practice is only "best" in situations where it will work. The same practice will not work in every situation.

4. Data is useful, but only if it is collected, analyzed, and used effectively. To be able to use data effectively in applying it to solutions, we must be able and willing to disaggregate it appropriately. For example, when people use the broad-brush expression, "Our schools are failing," what exactly does that mean? Are *all* schools failing? (No—our nation boasts many public schools that cannot possibly be defined as "failing," and to say otherwise is preposterous.) If we think a school is failing, in what *way* is it failing? What does the data say? Do we say a school is failing because the students' test scores in reading are lower than those of kids in other neighborhoods? Is the dropout rate too high? Are too many of the school's

graduates unemployed? And if they are unemployed, is the problem the school or lack of jobs in the community? If too many students are absent from school, is it because they're lazy, or is the neighborhood unsafe, or does school not seem relevant to them because they see no future other than flipping burgers?

5. When the problems are clearly defined, the solutions become goal oriented. The key is to be open-minded about the goals that we, as a nation, wish to achieve with our schools and our students. Should a goal be a certain score on a math test? If so, should the math test measure rote learning or the ability to be creative? Should a goal of a school be to *graduate* or to *educate*? The choice is not as simple as it may seem; if you make the goal to graduate, then you run the risk of kids being put ahead each year just to make the school's graduation rate look good. Or students who drop out are falsely recorded as having transferred to another school, thus rendering the data worthless.

If the process of identifying problems, finding solutions, and agreeing on goals seems much more complicated than the "*do something*" approach of the past sixty years—you're right, it is more complicated. That's why the one-size-fits-all solution has failed in the past and will fail again in the future. To make our schools the very best they can be (you'll notice that I did not say "to fix our schools"), we need a process that is fresh, unbiased, and open to every possibility.

PART THREE: THE PATH TO THE BEST POSSIBLE SCHOOLS

Separating Fact from Fiction

For sixty years, a bedrock axiom of the "do something" movement has been that our nation's public schools are bad.

Not underperforming in certain specific areas, but generally terrible in every way, everywhere.

Really? Does the wealthiest and most powerful nation in the history of human civilization actually have such terrible public schools?

If so, how did we put a man on the moon? How did we become a leader in digital technology? How could we have created the most advanced military weapons the world has ever seen? How did we send a satellite to Pluto?

The thing about condemning all public schools is that it allows you to sidestep the issue of inequality.

In fact, objective studies show that many of our nation's public schools are very good. Excellent, in fact. You just have to know where to find them.

School Rank and School Spending

Many organizations publish rankings of all types of schools—colleges, charter schools, private schools, public schools. One

161

such list is published by *U.S. News and World Report.* For its 2015 report, the magazine looks at a variety of indices, including:

1. Whether each school's students were performing better than statistically expected for students in their state. *U.S. News* started by looking at reading and math results for all students on each state's high school proficiency tests. They then factored in the percentages of economically disadvantaged students—who they say tend to score lower—enrolled at the schools to identify schools performing much better than statistical expectations.

2. For schools passing this first step, the second step assessed whether their disadvantaged students—black, Hispanic, and low-income—were outperforming similarly disadvantaged students in the state.

3. Schools that made it through the first two steps became eligible to be judged nationally on the final step—college-readiness performance—using Advanced Placement or International Baccalaureate test data as the benchmarks for success, depending on which program was largest at the school.

According to *U.S. News,* in 2015 these were the top fifteen public high schools in the United States:

1. School for the Talented and Gifted
   Dallas, Texas, Independent School District

2. BASIS Scottsdale
   Scottsdale, Arizona

3. Thomas Jefferson High School for
   Science and Technology
   Fairfax County, Virginia, Public Schools

4. Gwinnett School of Mathematics,
   Science and Technology
   Gwinnett County, Georgia, Public Schools

5. School of Science and Engineering Magnet
   Dallas, Texas, Independent School District

6. Carnegie Vanguard High School
   Houston, Texas, Independent School District

7. Academic Magnet High School
   Charleston County, South Carolina, School District

8. University High School
   Tolleson, Arizona, Union High School District

9. Lamar Academy
   McAllen, Texas

10. Gilbert Classical Academy High School
    Gilbert, Arizona, Unified District

11. The High School of American Studies
    at Lehman College
    New York City, New York, Public Schools

12. American Indian Public High School
    Oakland, California, School District

13. International Studies Charter High School
    Miami–Dade County, Florida, Public Schools

14. High School for Dual Language and Asian Studies
    New York City, New York, Public Schools

15. Northside College Preparatory High School
    Chicago, Illinois, Public Schools

The list is interesting for many reasons, but chiefly among them is the fact that these top schools are located in many big cities: New York, Miami, Chicago, Dallas. It's these urban school districts that are so often the targets of reformers like the producers of *Waiting for Superman*.

What does a top school look like?

To take one example, let's look at Northside College Prep in Chicago. Admission to Northside Prep follows the selective enrollment application system. Factors considered in the application include a student's grades from seventh grade, standardized test scores, entrance exam scores, and socioeconomic status. According to the *2014 Illinois School Report Card* published by the *Chicago Tribune*, the demographic makeup of Northside Prep's 1,055 students was 40.6% white, 17.7% Asian, 25.3% Hispanic, 8.7% black, 7.1% multiracial/ethnic, and .6% Native American or Native Hawaiian. Of the school's students, 37.3% were low income and 1.3% were homeless.

To put this in context, according to a 2014 report by Chicago's WBEZ 91.5 radio, the percentage of students in Chicago Public Schools who are considered low income has remained relatively stable since 2000, at about 86 percent. And two-thirds of the state's low-income kids now live *outside* the city.

"Every year we have been adding Title I [federal poverty] schools," said Jane Westerhold, superintendent of District 62, in Des Plaines, a Chicago suburb. "Even our schools that have typically been the more affluent schools in our neighborhoods are now also seeing that they qualify for Title I funding."

Des Plaines schools have also become more Latino, another statewide trend. In 2014, white students dipped under 50 percent of the public school population as a whole.

Westerhold told WBEZ she believed that much more than students' racial or ethnic backgrounds, it was poverty that is challenging schools. "It's not about our subgroups of students that are Hispanic students or Asian students or black students," she said. "It's really not about that. It's about poverty—that is where the achievement gap is."

Why is Northside successful? Perhaps because it's able to cherry-pick those students—regardless of income—who for whatever reason have *already* been successful in elementary and middle school. They're choosing the students who are classroom ready and exceed the average. Meanwhile, their average and below-average peers are left behind in their neighborhood schools.

It can be argued that despite being a part of the public school system, a school like Northside is not a typical public school precisely because it can *choose* its students. Meanwhile, the neighborhood public school must admit any noncriminal child in the district: the overachievers, the underachievers, the special needs kids, the kids who don't speak much English, the kids who are rich, and the kids who are poor. They cannot choose their student body. The administrators and teachers need to work with the students who walk through the door. They must *test* all the students who walk through the door—and those test results are used by government agencies to evaluate the school itself.

Therefore, rather than looking at individual public schools, it might make more sense to shine a light on individual school *districts.* A public school district generally includes several schools, and most, if not all, of them would be of the "open door" variety that must admit any qualified child. Are there, then, public school districts that are exceptional, and produce top students?

Yes, there are.

Many agencies and publications rank school districts. One of them is Niche.com, a public information website "that seeks to 'make choosing a neighborhood, college, or K–12 school a more transparent process.'"

Based on dozens of statistics and twenty-seven million opinions from three hundred thousand students and parents, Niche.com ranks more than one hundred thousand public and private schools and districts. Its report entitled "2016 Best School Districts" ranked the top 100 public school districts in the United States. For each school district listed here, the demographic information is from US Census Bureau reports for the most recent available year. It's worth noting that in 2010—the last official census—the Great Recession still gripped many parts of the United States, and yet the poverty numbers for these school districts are very low.

The top five public school districts were:

1. **Tredyffrin-Easttown School District.** Tredyffrin Township, Chester County, Pennsylvania. The mean household income is $112,472. The percentage of families living below the federal poverty line is 2.5 percent.

2. **Eanes Independent School District.** Travis County,
   Texas. The school district encompasses the whole city
   of West Lake Hills, a majority of Rollingwood, the Lost
   Creek neighborhood, and parts of Austin including
   Davenport and the Cuernavaca neighborhoods.
   In West Lake Hills, the mean household income is
   $160,574. The percentage of families living below the
   federal poverty line is 4.7 percent.
   In Rollingwood, the mean household income is
   $161,429. The percentage of families living below the
   federal poverty line is 2.2 percent.

3. **Jericho Union Free School District (or Jericho
   UFSD).** Jericho, New York. The district contains three
   elementary schools, one middle school, and one high
   school. The mean household income is $137,463. The
   percentage of families living below the federal poverty
   line is 2.2 percent.

4. **New Trier High School (also known as New Trier
   Township High School or NTHS).** Winnetka Village,
   Illinois. A public four-year high school, with its main
   campus for sophomores through seniors located in
   Winnetka and a freshman campus in Northfield, Illinois,
   with freshman classes and district administration.
   In Winnetka Village, the mean household income is
   $207,540. The percentage of families living below the
   federal poverty line is 2.0 percent.

5. **Princeton Public Schools.** Princeton, New Jersey. The
   mean household income is $187,662. The percentage
   of families living below the federal poverty line is 3.0
   percent.

For the United States as a whole, the mean household income is $74,596. The percentage of families living below the federal poverty line is 11.5 percent.

Each one of these top five school districts enjoys a mean household income that is *far above* the US average, and a poverty rate that is *far below* the US average.

Does this mean that these school districts are ranked higher because the schools themselves have more money poured into them—money for computers, swimming pools, chemistry labs, teachers, coaches? It's undeniably a factor; you cannot operate a school under a tree, as Plato did. You need a clean, safe, well-equipped school for students to thrive in.

A valid question is this: How much do we spend per student in public school? According to the US Department of Education, from the school years 2000–01 to 2011–12, current expenditures per student enrolled in the fall in public elementary and secondary schools increased by 11 percent, from $9,904 to $11,014 in constant 2013–14 dollars. Current expenditures per student peaked in 2008–09 at $11,537 and have decreased each year since then. The amount for 2011–12 ($11,014) was 3 percent ($318) less than the amount for 2010–11 ($11,332).

According to the Niche.com report, the amounts spent per student by the top five schools are:

1. Tredyffrin-Easttown School District: $16,180.
2. Eanes Independent School District: $18,409.
3. Jericho Union Free School District: $34,007.
4. New Trier High School: $24,209.
5. Princeton Public Schools: $24,368.

As you go down the list of the top 100, there's not a lot of variation. Number 50 on the list, Acalanes Union High School District in Central Contra Costa Township, California, spends an average of $15,377 per student. Number 100 on the list, Port Washington Union Free School District in North Hempstead Town, New York, spends an average of $25,633 per student—more than four of the top five schools.

Spending per student is a complex issue. For example, according to 24/7WallSt.com, five of the ten highest spending districts are located in Alaska. These high-spending Alaskan districts range from moderately wealthy to poor. For example, the Yukon Flats district, which has a median annual household income of just $27,014—much lower than the national median of $53,046—still spends an average of $29,273 per student, the second most in the country. (The *median* income is the income that falls exactly in the center of the number of sample households. The *mean* income is the total income of all households divided by the number of households. The mean income is usually more affected by the relatively unequal distribution of income, which tilts toward the top. As a result, the mean tends to be higher than the *median* income, with the top-earning households boosting it. The *mean* household income in the US is $74,596.)

Michael Griffith, senior policy analyst with the Education Commission of the States, an education policy research group, told 24/7WallSt.com that the high spending in Alaska has to do in part with the state's unique, isolated geography, which raises the costs of everything from busing students to building maintenance costs. You simply have to pay more for *everything* in Alaska, including schools.

Is there a cause and effect relationship between school spending and student outcomes? It's not clear. As 24/7WallSt.com reported, spending alone does not determine student achievement. In five of the most poorly funded districts the report identified, graduation rates were in excess of 92 percent. In five of the best-funded states, less than 80 percent of a given class graduates high school. Sterling Lloyd, senior research associate at *Education Week*, explained, "There's no consensus in the research about the precise role of school spending for student achievement. It's a perennial debate. You can find studies that indicate there is a relationship between funding and student achievement, and you can find studies that say there isn't a relationship. There really isn't any consensus in the field."

The International Context

Amid the shrill calls to "do something" and the sensationalist films, there are cool-headed voices of reason. In January 2015, the Horace Mann League (HML) and the National Superintendents Roundtable released their report entitled "School Performance in Context: The Iceberg Effect." The report examined six dimensions related to student performance—equity, social stress, support for families, support for schools, student outcomes, and system outcomes—in the G-7 nations (Canada, France, Germany, Italy, Japan, the United Kingdom, and the United States) plus Finland and China. They then examined twenty-four "indicators" within those dimensions.

The study was a groundbreaking analysis that compared K–12 education internationally on an array of social and economic indicators, not just test scores. The goal was to look at the whole iceberg, not just the tip—and provide a clearer snapshot of each country's performance, including its wealth, diversity, community safety, and support for families and schools.

The report revealed that the US, which remains the wealthiest of the nine nations, has the most highly educated workforce, based on the number of years of school completed and the proportion of adults with high school diplomas and bachelor's degrees.

The US leads the nine-nation group in spending per student, although the report cautions that national estimates may not be truly comparable. American teachers spend about 40 percent more time in the classroom than their peers in the comparison countries.

In educational levels of its adult workforce, the US leads these nine nations. American students also make up 25 percent of the world's top students in science at age fifteen, followed by Japan at 13 percent.

"Many policymakers and business leaders fret that America has fallen behind Europe and China, but our research does not bear that out," said James Harvey, executive director of the National Superintendents Roundtable.

Despite the overall positive findings, the report cited some significant challenges. The US is one of the most diverse nations with many immigrant students, suggesting that for many students English may not be their first language. Within the US there are significant variations in levels of economic inequity, social stress, rates of childhood poverty, and violence. While all nations demonstrate an achievement gap based on students' family income and socioeconomic status, of the nine nations surveyed, the United States and China demonstrated the greatest gaps between rich and poor. The US also showed high rates of income inequality and childhood poverty. Rates of violent death are thirteen times greater than the average for the other nations, with children in some communities reporting they have witnessed shootings, knifings, and beatings as "ordinary, everyday events." The United States showed the highest rates of teen pregnancy and violent death, and came in second for death rates from drug abuse.

You might think that in the richest nation on earth, such statistics would spur federal spending on social and economic issues. But the US appeared in the lowest third on public spending for services that benefit children and families, including preschool.

"Too often, we narrow our focus to a few things that can be easily tested," said Gary Marx, president of the Horace Mann League. "To avoid that scoreboard mentality, we need to look at many measures important to shaping our future citizens. Treating education as a horse race doesn't work."

The report noted, "American policymakers from both political parties have a history of relying on large, international assessments to judge United States' performance in education. In 2013, the press reported that American students were falling behind when compared to 61 other countries and a few cities including Shanghai. In that comparative assessment—called the Program for International Student Assessment—PISA controversially reported superior scores for Shanghai. 'We don't oppose using international assessments as one measure of performance. But as educators and policymakers, we need to compare ourselves with similar nations and on a broader set of indicators that put school performance in context—not just a single number in an international ranking,' said James Harvey, executive director of the National Superintendents Roundtable."

HML Executive Director Jack McKay said, "Our study suggests the US has the most educated workforce, yet students confront shockingly high rates of poverty and violence. Research shows that those larger issues, outside the classroom, are serious threats to student learning."

That bears repeating: It is the larger issues, *outside the classroom*, that impede student learning.

In making comparisons to foreign countries like Finland and even individual cities like Shanghai, the "do something" advocates too often compare America's diverse population—which includes low-income children and immigrants who speak little English— with the homogeneous populations of countries like Finland, Japan, and New Zealand. As Hal Salzman and Lindsay Lowell wrote in their 2008 article for *Nature*, average performance tells us nothing about the distribution of students with the best test scores. "In maths and science," they wrote, "when looking at average scores, the United States is outranked by countries such as Finland and South Korea. But the rankings change when we examine the percentage of students who perform at the top, those most likely to be tomorrow's innovators. The South Korean average places it in the top-ranked group of nations, yet its relative proportion of top-performing students is 30% lower than that of the United States. In fact, the United States has a higher percentage of top-performing students than five of the fourteen others in the top-ranked group of countries with high average scores."

In their 2013 report for the Economic Policy Institute entitled "What do international tests really show about U.S. student performance?" researchers Martin Carnoy and Richard Rothstein caution that using average test scores to draw conclusions about how American students stand up against foreign students is highly misleading. "Because academic performance differences are produced by home and community as well as school influences," they wrote, "there is an achievement gap between the relative average performance of students from higher and lower social classes in every industrialized nation. Thus, for a valid assessment of how well American schools perform, policymakers should compare the performance of U.S. students with that of students in other countries who have been and are being shaped by approximately similar home and community environments... Policymakers and school reformers may acknowledge these realities, but frequently proceed to ignore them in practice, denouncing relative U.S. international test performance with sweeping generalizations that make no attempt to compare students from similar social class positions."

The United States is a big country with great diversity, and our best students are as accomplished as the best students anywhere in the world. This suggests that our *basic approach* to public education is not broken, since the basic approach is the same in every public school. The biggest difference may lie not with the schools themselves but with the communities that support those schools.

As Paul Farhi wrote in the *American Journalism Review* in May 2012, the national media, in its coverage of the supposed crisis in America's public schools, has rarely looked closely at the effect of poverty and class, the single greatest variable in educational achievement. "Academic research," wrote Farhi, "has shown for many years that poor children, or those born to parents who are poorly educated themselves, don't do as well in school as better-off students. More recent work by, among others, Sean

F. Reardon of Stanford University, suggests that the achievement gap between rich and poor children has grown wider since the 1960s, reflecting in part the nation's growing economic disparity. The problem is vast—some 22 percent of American children live in poverty, the highest among Western democracies."

The Persistence of Misinformation

How do you measure the success or failure of a school or a school system?

What yardstick do you use?

Minimum test scores? Year-over-year test score improvement? Graduation rates? Attendance rates? How many graduates go on to higher education? How many graduates get good jobs? How many of the school's students stay out of jail?

Let's look at one metric, the numbers of graduates, and how even this can be misleading. For example, a key claim by the "do something" people is that China and India are graduating tens of thousands more engineers than the United States, and the gap is so great this is a problem of national security.

For example, on July 25, 2005, the American public school system was slammed with yet another "Sputnik moment." *Fortune* magazine ran a cover showing a brawny China bullying a scrawny Uncle Sam on the beach—a parody of the old Charles Atlas comic book body building ads. The cover story was entitled "Is the U.S. a 97-Pound Weakling?" We're losing our competitive edge, the article stated, while citing these three numbers: 600,000, 350,000, and 70,000. These were, allegedly, the number of engineers produced in 2004 in China, India, and the United States, respectively.

The figures were unsubstantiated, but they quickly became embedded in the popular psyche.

In October 2005, the Committee on Science, Engineering, and Public Policy, a joint group from the National Academy of Sciences, National Academy of Engineering, and Institute of Medicine (which, with the National Research Council, are collectively known as the National Academies), published a press release in advance of its 543-page report called "Rising Above the Gathering Storm," an allusion to Winston Churchill's book *The Gathering Storm*, about events leading up to World War II. The press release stated, "Last year more than 600,000 engineers graduated from institutions of higher education in China. In India the figure was 350,000. In America, it was about 70,000."

In May 2006, *Washington Post* reporter Gerald W. Bracey did some fact checking on these three numbers. He wrote, "The statistics then materialized in *The New York Times, Boston Globe, Chicago Tribune* and on many Web sites. While *Times* columnist Thomas L. Friedman did not use these specific numbers in his 2005 bestseller, *The World Is Flat*, he did write that Asian universities currently produce eight times as many bachelor's degrees in engineering as U.S. universities do.

"Carl Bialik, who writes the 'Numbers Guy' column in the *Wall Street Journal*, was suspicious," continued Bracey. "He had previously examined the *Fortune* numbers and concluded that they were inflated, so he sought to find their source. The most likely origin for the 600,000 Chinese engineers was a 2002 speech by Ray Bingham, then-chief executive of a semiconductor company. Bialik couldn't find any obvious birthplace for the Indian figures, but National Science Foundation analysts told him the number was unlikely to be anywhere near 350,000."

Bracey tracked down the 2004 *China Statistical Yearbook*, issued by the Chinese government, which reported that China produced 644,000 engineering graduates that year. But the yearbook is only a compilation of numbers sent by the heads of provincial governments (who would *never* lie to Beijing, of course!). The accuracy of these provincial reports could not be verified, and even the definition of an "engineer" in China is vague. A McKinsey study of nine occupations, including engineering, concluded that "fewer than ten percent of Chinese job candidates, on average, would be suitable for work [in a multinational company] in the nine occupations we studied."

On December 12, 2005, Duke University researchers Vivek Wadhwa and G. Gereffi published their report entitled "Framing the Engineering Outsourcing Debate," in which they examined these numbers. They wrote, "Varying, inconsistent reporting of problematic, engineering graduation data has been used to fuel fears that America is losing its technological edge. Typical articles have stated that in 2004 the United States graduated roughly 70,000 undergraduate engineers, while China graduated 600,000 and India 350,000. Our study has determined that these are inappropriate comparisons.

"These massive numbers of Indian and Chinese engineering graduates include not only four-year degrees, but also three-year training programs and diploma holders. These numbers have been compared against the annual production of accredited four-year engineering degrees in the United States.

"In addition to the lack of nuanced analysis around the type of graduates (transactional or dynamic) and quality of degrees being awarded, these articles also tend not to ground the numbers in the larger demographics of each country. A comparison of like-to-like data suggests that the U.S. produces a highly significant number of engineers, computer scientists and information technology specialists, and remains competitive in global markets."

They found that the United States annually produces 137,437 engineers with at least a bachelor's degree, while India produces 112,000 and China 351,537. That's more US degrees per million residents than in either India or China.

Furthermore, as Vivek Wadhwa wrote for *Bloomberg News*, "The quality of these [Chinese] engineers, however, is so poor that most are not fit to work as engineers; their system of rote learning handicaps those who do get jobs, so it takes two to three years for them to achieve the same productivity as fresh American graduates. As a result, significant proportions of China's engineering graduates end up working on factory floors, and Indian industry has to spend large sums of money retraining its employees. After four or five years in the workforce, Indians do become innovative and produce, overall, at the same quality as Americans, but they lose a valuable two to three years in their retraining." In short, what they call an "engineer" is more like what we would call an "apprentice."

Yet despite being repeatedly debunked, the myth of the 600,000 persisted!

On December 5, 2011, *The New York Times* published a brief essay by Kai-Fu Leeduc, the former head of Google China and the founder of Innovation Works, a Chinese incubator and investment firm. The essay, entitled "China Is Poised for an I.T. Golden Age," delivered this scary news: "Chinese universities graduate more than 600,000 engineering students a year. China has consistently placed at or near the top of programming competitions. And while we have not seen China become a leader in information technology and computing, I expect that this will change in the coming decade."

Leeduc then went on to say that in China, many companies have become successful by taking American ideas and localizing them for China. These companies may have "copied" (or perhaps less charitably, stolen) technology from the United States, but subsequently focused on their customers and developed their products with local innovations.

He concluded his essay by saying, "In a country full of energy, desire, talent and ideas, there is no doubt that China will become a world leader in information technology."

Like a Sputnik moment that becomes a Sputnik decade, the specter of hordes of well-trained Chinese and Indian engineers has been used by proponents of charter schools and vouchers to "prove" that American public schools are failing when, in fact, our best public schools are more than a match for any public school anywhere else on the planet.

Why? Why is there a persistent belief that American public schools are universally lousy?

Perhaps it's because that with the singular exception of the US military—whose annual budget of $581 billion is larger than the next nine nations *combined*—many Americans are convinced that whatever the government does must be shoddy. Public schools are crummy simply because they are operated by government bureaucrats in collusion with public sector unions, and therefore a public school could not possibly be as good as any privately owned school.

It's as simple as that. Many people believe that if the government is involved in something, it's got to be lousy and a waste of money. For this reason we should bust the unions, encourage private and charter schools, give poor families vouchers so they can ship their kids across town to "better" schools, and demand that the kids left behind in neighborhood schools haul themselves up by their own bootstraps.

The idea of using federal money for private school vouchers and other education alternatives has long appealed to advocates of privatization, but the recent spurt in new voucher programs in states has encouraged lawmakers in Congress who have a bleak view of public schools.

In 2015, US Senator Lamar Alexander (R-Tenn.), a former governor and education secretary under President George H. W. Bush, proposed a bill that would allow low-income students to use federal tax dollars to pay for private school tuition.

"Our elementary and secondary education system is not the best in the world," he said. "U.S. fifteen-year-olds rank 28th in science and 36th in math. I believe one reason for this is that while more than 93 percent of federal dollars spent for higher education follow students to colleges of their choice, federal dollars do not automatically follow K–12 students to schools of their choice. Instead, money is sent directly to schools," Alexander said. "Local government monopolies run most schools and tell most students which school to attend. There is little choice and no K–12 marketplace as there is in higher education."

Opponents argued against Alexander's proposal, saying that it would divert scarce dollars meant for the country's poorest students to private schools.

His bill was narrowly defeated.

Critics, including teachers unions and groups such as the National School Boards Association, say "school choice" sounds good but can pour tax dollars into private hands with little accountability and uncertain educational outcomes.

Low-Performing Schools

Given that the American public school system is extremely diverse, and that in middle income, upper income, and affluent communities our approach to public education can produce top-quality high school graduates, it makes sense to focus our attention on schools that are located in low-income communities and which, for whatever reason, struggle to educate their students. Our first task is to determine what a low-performing school looks like. What measurement are we going to use? Let's start with what the US government says.

According to the US Department of Education, low-performing schools are those in the bottom 10 percent of performance in a given state, or who have significant achievement gaps, based on student academic performance in reading/language arts and mathematics on assessments required under the ESEA or graduation rates.

As Richard C. Seder wrote in "Balancing Accountability and Local Control: State Intervention for Financial and Academic Stability" in 2000, states customarily categorize schools as "low-performing" or "falling" by virtue of persistently subpar scores on standardized tests, sometimes along with low graduation and high dropout rates.

In Massachusetts, according to the Massachusetts Budget and Policy Center, "The state defines underperforming schools (Level 4) as being in the bottom 20 percent of all schools statewide. Chronically underperforming schools (Level 5) are underperforming schools that fail to improve with a turnaround plans over several years."

To rate its schools, Georgia has created the College and Career Ready Performance Index (CCRPI). Concurrently, the Georgia Private School Tax Credit Law (O.C.G.A. § 20-2A) allows student scholarship organizations (SSOs) to provide scholarships for eligible students to attend accredited private schools. House Bill 283 (2013) waived the enrollment and six-week public school attendance eligibility requirements for those students who have been assigned to a "low-performing school." The bill also requires the Governor's Office of Student Achievement (GOSA) to determine a list of "low-performing schools" for this specific purpose. This definition of "low-performing school" is solely intended to determine eligibility for SSO scholarships.

The Governor's Office of Student Achievement (GOSA) defines a "low-performing school" as a school that has a score that falls at or below the 25th percentile in its grade cluster (elementary, middle, and high school clusters).

Based on 2013–2014 CCRPI scores, schools with the following scores are "low performing schools" for the purposes of this law:

Elementary schools: 2013–2014 CCRPI score of 65.9 or less.
Middle schools: 2013–2014 CCRPI score of 67.5 or less.
High schools: 2013–2014 CCRPI score of 60.8 or less.

Presumably, this means, for example, that a high school with a CCRPI score of 61 would pass, while a school with a score of 60 would be labeled as "low performing." You can imagine the pressure on a school principal to get the score of his or her school up by one point!

The use of one numerical score to "grade" an entire school has not gone unquestioned. Matt Underwood, executive director of Atlanta Neighborhood Charter School (ANCS), wrote in the ANCS blog On Education, "And so, as you might imagine, I see some problems with Georgia's new 'College and Career Ready Performance Index' (CCRPI), a single numeric score—on a scale of 0–100—given to each public school in Georgia and that will be used, according to the Georgia Department of Education, to 'hold schools accountable and reward them for the work they do in all subjects and with all students'... Other states who are using single scores or grades for schools have encountered challenges from research showing the shortcomings of such systems to charges that the formula used to tabulate the grades were changed to improve grades for certain schools. New York City is doing away with assigning schools with letter grades entirely because a single grade or score—devoid of context—provides little meaningful information and mainly sparks ill-informed conversations about and comparisons between schools."

Any data point yardstick can give a misleading measurement, and schools that admirably serve their low-income communities can be arbitrarily labeled as "underperforming." In February 2003, *The New York Times* profiled the Porfirio H. Gonzales Elementary School in Tolleson, Arizona. Reporter Michael Winerip wrote that the students, the parents, and teachers believed they had a terrific school. This was despite the fact that the mostly Mexican-American student body was very poor (83 percent received free lunches), Spanish was the first language of half the children, many were migrants, and the school's annual mobility rate was 29 percent—typically, signs of a very challenging education environment.

The school has children with parents in prison and students who sleep four to a bed. Yet on national and state tests that measured a student's yearly academic progress, this poor school scored above average.

To these first- and second-generation immigrant families, Gonzales Elementary represented America's promise and her generosity: a free breakfast program, an after-school program and a health clinic, with a dental clinic soon to be added. In a survey, 88 percent of parents gave the school an A or B. They loved their principal, Jim Paxinos, an Anglo who spoke Spanish, worked twelve-hour days, lived nearby, and learned his profession by teaching in inner-city Phoenix.

Under the No Child Left Behind Act, states could rate schools solely on how much the student body improved on math and English competency tests. The fact that one hundred transient students may have been at Gonzales Elementary for just a few months when they took the tests was not a mitigating factor. Nor did it matter that hundreds had serious deficiencies in English.

If they scored low, it was the school's fault. Period.

In 2002 the fifth grade did not make adequate progress on the state competency exams. And that's all it took for the school to be labeled "underperforming," and by the following fall, in all likelihood, it would be labeled "failing."

Along with principals at Arizona's other 274 "underperforming" schools, Principal Jim Paxinos was summoned to Phoenix for an audience with the state bureaucracy. "They told us the law requires us to submit a school improvement plan," Paxinos told *The New York Times.* "One principal asked, 'Who will evaluate the plan?' The woman from the state laughed. She said, 'We don't have the resources.'"

By all accounts, the "improvement plan" that Principal Paxinos dutifully submitted ended up in the bottom of a filing cabinet.

The Coleman Report

The idea that schools reflect their communities is not new. In 1966, James Samuel Coleman, an American sociologist, theorist, and empirical researcher at the University of Chicago, published "Equality of Educational Opportunity," commonly known as the "Coleman Report." US Commissioner of Education Harold Howe commissioned Coleman and several other scholars at Johns Hopkins University to write a report on educational equality in the United States. One of the largest studies in history, it included more than 650,000 students and teachers in its samples. The report focused on this question: which strategy was more likely to equalize educational opportunities for poor minority students—racial integration or compensatory education? (Compensatory education is the provision of supplementary programs or services designed to help children at risk of cognitive impairment and low educational achievement succeed.)

Coleman's report reached two conclusions.

1. Racial integration did little to boost academic achievement in urban schools. "Our interpretation of the data," Coleman wrote, "is that racial integration per se is unrelated to achievement insofar as the data can show a relationship."

2. Compensatory education—whether offered in racially integrated or in racially segregated schools—was similarly unlikely to improve achievement levels. As Coleman explained, "Differences in school facilities and curricula, which are made to improve schools, are so little related to differences in achievement levels of

students that, with few exceptions, their efforts [or the effects of different classes or curricula] fail to appear in a survey of this magnitude."

Further studies suggested that the best way to improve academic achievement was neither to integrate students nor to offer compensatory programs but, rather, to raise overall family income. According to the work of sociologist David Armor, as cited by the US Department of Education, "Programs which stress financial aid to disadvantaged black families may be just [as] important, if not more so, than programs aimed at integrating blacks into white neighborhoods and schools."

Another study concluded that the "racial composition of the school... does not have a substantial effect [on academic achievement]—not nearly so strong as the social class composition of the school." In other words, when it came to improving academic achievement in the inner city, what mattered most was neither special programs nor racial integration but, rather, family background and socioeconomic status.

The report concluded that school funding had little effect on student achievement, and that student background and socioeconomic status were more important in determining educational outcomes of a student. Additionally, the report found that differences in the quality of schools and teachers had a small positive impact on student outcomes.

"The Family: America's Smallest School"

In 2007, the principles of the Coleman Report were echoed in a report published by the Educational Testing Service entitled "The Family: America's Smallest School." Authors Paul E. Barton and Richard J. Coley asserted that the family and the home are both critical education institutions where children begin learning long before they start school, and where they spend much of their time after school. So it stood to reason that in order to improve the educational achievement of the nation's students and close the achievement gaps, a critical step would be to improve home environments and make them more conducive to learning. To back up their thesis, the authors presented an analysis using six family/home conditions that had been shown to be linked to student achievement. The six conditions were:

1. The parent-pupil ratio. The report stated that the percentage of two-parent families has been in long-term decline. Single-parent families are rapidly becoming a significant segment of the country's family population.
2. Family finances. Income is an important factor in a family's ability to fund the tangible and intangible elements that contribute to making the home an educationally supportive environment.
3. Literacy development. Literacy development begins long before children enter formal education, and is critical to their success in school.
4. Child care disparities. The availability of high-quality child care is critical when parents work outside the home.
5. The home as an educational resource. The resources available at home—books, magazines, newspapers, a home computer with access to the Internet, a quiet place for study—can have a lasting influence on a child's ability to achieve academically.

6. The parent-school relationship. A significant body of research indicates that when parents, teachers, and schools work together to support learning, students do better in school and stay in school longer. Parental involvement in student education includes everything from making sure children do their homework, to attending school functions and parent-teacher conferences, to serving as an advocate for the school, to working in the classroom.

The authors distilled information about these conditions into what they called "four factors" that influence children's cognitive development and school performance. These factors tend to be interrelated and rarely exist in isolation from one another. These four factors are:

1. Parent-student ratio: The percentage of children under age eighteen who live with one parent.
2. Absenteeism: The percentage of eighth-graders who miss three or more days in a single month.
3. Reading to young children: The percentage of children age five or younger whose parents read to them every day.
4. Excessive television watching: The percentage of eighth-graders who watch five or more hours of television on a school day.

"Together," wrote the authors, "these four factors account for about two-thirds of the large differences among states in National Assessment of Educational Progress (NAEP) eighth-grade reading scores."

The report concluded, "The nation has set high goals for raising student achievement. Schools play a critical role in this effort, and it is appropriate that a serious national effort is being made to improve them. However, family characteristics and home environment play critical roles as well. Reaching our ambitious national goals will require serious efforts to address issues on both fronts."

The Way Forward

After sixty years of experiencing the cycle of education spending, testing, and hand-wringing, and by paying attention to objective studies, I think we can agree on a set of facts.

- We have established that, in general, American public schools are not failing. When data is disaggregated, students in public schools in middle income, upper income, and wealthy communities are performing as well as the best foreign students.
- We have established that in the case of low-performing schools, which are most often located in low-income communities, student achievement is not the problem; it is the outcome of other problems that are often rooted outside the school, beyond the schoolyard.
- We have established that because of the tremendous diversity of America's public schools, there cannot be a one-size-fits-all solution. It is pointless to apply the same set of standards to a school in a wealthy neighborhood as a school in a distressed neighborhood.
- We have established that problems are contextual and therefore are different for every school.

- We have established that the problems are more social/affective than cognitive.
- We have established that blindly "doing something" is not the most effective solution.
- We have established that money alone is not the answer—or at the very least, that money is being spent ineffectively.

This book is not just about changing federal policy toward education. It's also about practical, real-life solutions to problems that have plagued some of our nation's toughest schools. It's about taking a hard, realistic look at one school at a time—the school in your neighborhood—and going beyond the schoolyard to tackle the conditions that lead to poor performance in the classroom.

Marva Collins and the Collins Way

If you look hard enough, you'll find plenty of stories about educators who didn't wait around for Superman and who looked beyond the schoolyard for solutions. One of them was Marva Collins, who passed away in 2015 at the age of seventy-eight.

In 1975, after having worked as a substitute teacher for fourteen years in Chicago public schools, Marva Collins cashed in her $5,000 in pension savings and opened Westside Preparatory School. The school originally operated in the basement of a local college and then, to be free of bureaucratic red tape, in the second floor of her own home on Chicago's South Side. Collins made a point of not accepting federal funds because she did not want to be restricted by the regulations that came with such backing.

Charging eighty dollars a month in tuition, she began with four students, including her daughter. Enrollment at the school soon grew to more than two hundred, in classes from prekindergarten through eighth grade. The school remained in operation for more than thirty years.

Collins emphasized discipline, set high academic standards, and above all, she never expected her students to fail.

The Collins Method, as it came to be known, centered on math, reading, phonics, English, and the classics. Plato, Homer, Geoffrey Chaucer, and Leo Tolstoy were all part of the reading list. "People ask me, 'How do you get the children to memorize *The Canterbury Tales* in Old English?" Collins said. "I say, 'It never dawned on me that they couldn't learn it.' Kids don't fail. Teachers fail, school systems fail. The people who teach children that they are failures, they are the problem."

She told an interviewer, "We're an anomaly in a world of negatives. Our children are self-motivated, self-generating, self-propelled." At Westside Prep, "there are no dropouts, no substitute teachers, and when teachers are absent, the students teach themselves."

The implicit "flip side" to setting high expectations for students is that if you believe that all students are teachable, then it's your responsibility as a teacher to unlock their learning potential. You can't just say, "Oh, Johnny can't read. It's his fault." No—it becomes your responsibility to figure out how Johnny can learn. And guess what? A one-size-fits-all solution will never work. Human beings are complex creatures. Every student is unique, and every student brings his or her own abilities and challenges to the classroom. An approach that worked with Suzy may not work with Johnny.

In 1977, an article about the school in the *Chicago Sun-Times* attracted national attention. She was later the subject of a *60 Minutes* segment and of *The Marva Collins Story*, a 1981 television movie on CBS with Cicely Tyson playing Ms. Collins, and Morgan Freeman as her husband.

As her stature as an educator grew, she began to train other teachers from around the country and published several books, including *"Ordinary" Children, Extraordinary Teachers*, written with Civia Tamarkin. By 1991, Collins was training a thousand teachers each year on her methods of instilling pupils with a love of learning and an ability to think critically through classic literature. During that time, the school received about six thousand visitors annually who wanted to know "how we make scholars of children at a time when people lament that nothing can be done," Collins told the *Chicago Tribune* that year.

In 1980, President-elect Ronald Reagan was said to be leaning toward choosing Ms. Collins for secretary of education, but she said she would reject the job if it were offered. She had already turned down offers to run the public school systems in Chicago and Los Angeles.

In 2008, due to a lack of resources and falling enrollment, Westside Preparatory School closed its doors. But with thousands of her students placed in jobs and attending colleges around the country, Collins's impact on the American school system, and the many lives she helped improve, continues.

Jaime Alfonso Escalante Gutierrez

Jaime Alfonso Escalante Gutierrez, who passed away in 2010, was a Bolivian-born educator known for teaching students calculus from 1974 to 1991 at Garfield High School, East Los Angeles, California. Escalante was the subject of the 1988 film

Stand and Deliver, in which he was portrayed by the actor Edward James Olmos.

Escalante taught mathematics and physics for twelve years in Bolivia before immigrating to the United States. In 1974, he got a job teaching at Garfield High School, a rundown school known for violence and drugs. "They were using their fingers adding stuff at the board," Escalante told *People Weekly* in April of 1988. "They came in without supplies, with nothing. Total chaos." Escalante believed that his first year at Garfield would be his last.

While many had dismissed the students as "unteachable," Escalante strove to reach his students and to encourage them to live up to their potential. In the fall of 1975, Garfield High was in danger of losing its accreditation. Escalante believed that teachers should challenge students rather than teach at the lowest level possible. With a new administration in place, Escalante was able to advocate for more challenging classes. He began teaching algebra, and by 1979 he introduced the first calculus class at Garfield.

Escalante promised his hesitant students that they could get good jobs in engineering, electronics, and computers, but they would have to learn math to succeed. He told them, "I'll teach you math and that's your language. With that you're going to make it. You're going to college and sit in the first row, not the back, because you're going to know more than anybody."

Eventually Escalante's math enrichment program grew to over four hundred students. His class sizes increased to over fifty students in some cases. In 1991, the number of Garfield students taking advanced placement examinations in math and other subjects jumped to five hundred and seventy. That same year, Escalante and fellow math teacher Ben Jiménez left Garfield.

Escalante found new employment at Hiram W. Johnson High School in Sacramento, California.

At the height of Escalante's influence, Garfield graduates were said to be entering the University of Southern California in such great numbers that they outnumbered all the other high schools in the working-class East Los Angeles region combined. Even students who failed the AP went on to become star students at California State University, Los Angeles, in large numbers.

Like Marva Collins, Jaime Escalante understood that teaching is a one-on-one business. There is no one-size-fits-all solution. He also knew the importance of going beyond the schoolyard. To prepare his students for the AP test, he held special after-school sessions and Saturday classes. During their lunch hour or before classes began, he tutored students who were struggling. Most importantly, he got the parents involved and convinced them to make their children attend school and do their homework. As he told the *Omaha World-Herald* in April of 2001, "We need the help of parents. We alone cannot do anything."

"I am not looking for recognition," he told the *Los Angeles Times* in May of 1995. "I'm trying to prove that potential is anywhere and we can teach any kid if we have the *ganas* (desire) to do it."

Gresham Park Elementary School

They say that you should always write about what you know. It's in this spirit that I offer the following case study. I offer it not because I can claim to have accomplished anything exceptional on my own, but because I experienced firsthand the change that can happen when people work together toward a common goal. And

I offer it not because I'm wholly responsible for a good outcome; at any school, progress and improvement is always a collaborative effort among community stakeholders, administrators, teachers, parents, and students.

In 1996, I was appointed principal of Gresham Park Elementary School in DeKalb County, Georgia. DeKalb County is a large and diverse suburb of Atlanta.

At Gresham Park Elementary School, we served a particularly disadvantaged community. Here's a brief snapshot:

- Our students were 100% African American.
- They were predominantly low income, with 88% of our students qualifying for free or reduced-price lunch. In 2000–2001 the national average was 38.3 percent.
- Most of our students lived with a single parent or grandparent. Only 20% of our children lived in traditional two-parent homes.
- Many of our students and their parent(s) lived with a grandmother. The average age of a grandmother was thirty-six years old.
- The educational level of our parents was low. In the United States, roughly 90% of adults have a high school diploma. Among our student community, only 55% of parents had graduated from high school.
- Of the roughly one-third of parents who had a high school diploma, only 10% of that number had gone to college.
- Forty-five percent of our parents and grandparents were unemployed. In 1996, the year of my appointment, the national unemployment rate was 5.6 percent.

The school itself was in poor condition. It was very dirty, and cluttered with broken equipment and old books. When I first walked through the front door I smelled urine even though the bathroom was far down the hall. The walls were painted with what can charitably be called "prison grey," with additional profane graffiti.

The educational attainment of our students was low. Ninety percent of our students were served by Title I or EIP reading and math remedial programs. Ninety percent of our students scored below the 50th percentile on the ITBS test.

The school was experiencing a myriad of challenges, including low student attendance, low student achievement, and poor school community relations.

My team and I faced big challenges. We knew that Superman wasn't coming, and we also knew that slapping a coat of paint on the school and telling the students to shape up or ship out was not a solution. We had to go beyond the schoolyard and help our families build a foundation for learning at home and in the community. Without this solid foundation, we knew that anything we did in the school would be a waste of time and money.

In order to affect school improvement and turn around this failing school, we developed and implemented a number of innovative initiatives. We developed and followed a clearly defined Community Development Model.

Community Development Model:

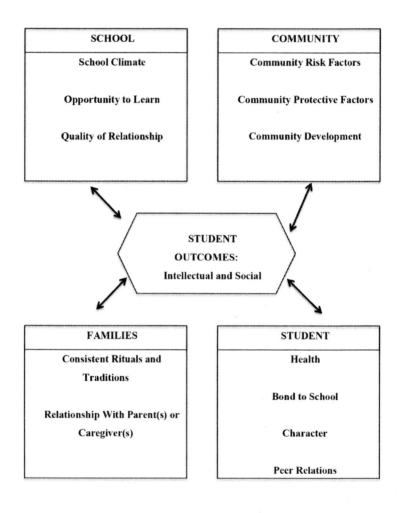

Step 1: Define the problem

In order to understand where our students were coming from, I first needed to go outside the schoolyard. I walked through the neighborhood, knocked on doors, and said, "Hi, I'm your new principal. Tell me what's wrong with our school and tell me how to fix it." You will note that I did not say, "Come to a meeting at school." If you say that, most parents won't come. They're working, or live too far away, or they're embarrassed because they have no job and they think they'll feel uncomfortable sitting among other parents. On my home visits I was amazed at how eager people were to "sound off." I learned a lot by going beyond the schoolyard and into our constituents' homes.

Students were given that same opportunity, as were the staff (this happened in school—I didn't visit every teacher at home!). Everyone had the chance to make their opinions and feelings known.

Step 2: Create internal structure, routine, and order by developing a staff handbook

We knew that our first job was to get our own house in order. We had to get our people thinking and acting professionally. A good teacher can teach in a cave. You make do with what you have. We knew that Superman wasn't coming, and we also knew that telling our students to enroll in a charter school was neither realistic nor fair. Our kids deserved to have a neighborhood public school that could provide a good education. And that starts with the people.

We developed a staff handbook, just like any other place of business would. It covered basic responsibilities: Our staff would get to work on time, dress appropriately, and complete all lesson plans. Perhaps most importantly, individually and collectively we would take responsibility for all of our children.

Step 3: Engage the community

Our mission was to go beyond the schoolyard, reach out to the community, and make sure that business owners and community leaders understood the importance of their neighborhood school. We solicited assistance from churches and from businesses in the area, including Chevron gas, Church's chicken, and even Bigalow's, a neighborhood bar.

Step 4: Develop safety nets and programs for students

Talking about connecting with the community wasn't enough. We knew that we had to provide actual programs and resources for our students and their families. These included:

- Our SLAM program (math assistance and reading assistance after school and on Saturdays).
- We partnered with Southside Hospital, which provided a nurse for the school in addition to assisting with implementing community health fairs that provided health screening and other services to residents and children of the community.
- For the governor's reading program we received $15,000 from the governor's discretionary fund to purchase more books and reading material for students.
- We developed the Discovery-Based Reading Program, included a reading curriculum that was centered around nursery rhymes, fairy tales, fables, and the classics. Students were excited about school again.
- We partnered with the Georgia Division of Family

and Children Services (DFCS) to assist parents with obtaining state or federal assistance when they qualified.

- We partnered with a local retirement center to have the elderly come out and read to the students and mentor them.
- We developed a GED program to help adults obtain their high school diplomas.
- We worked with the local police department to shut down the known drug houses.
- We instituted a monthly cleanup day at school.
- We started a school drama program, where students were cast in plays to develop and showcase their talents.
- We developed the Family Technology Resource Center (FTRC), which provided computer training to parents in the community in the evening after normal school hours. Parents were trained in the use of Windows and the Microsoft Office Suite, including Word, Excel, and PowerPoint. Parents who participated in the program were expected to provide a number of volunteer hours to the school. I also worked with want ads to assist them in obtaining jobs.

Step 5: Assess, review, and revisit

The results were overwhelming. During my tenure as principal, student achievement as measured by standardized test scores improved significantly, student attendance showed a significant improvement, and parental participation and community relations also improved significantly.

Our efforts were noticed by the wider community. The Family Technology Resource Center received a Computer World award from the Smithsonian Institution, and I received a personal telephone call from then President Bill Clinton congratulating me on the improvements at the school. In addition, I received the M. L. King Jr. Humanitarian Award, the Presidential Award for Innovative Programs, and the John Stanford Award from the United States Department of Education. This award was presented in a ceremony in Washington, DC, by then Secretary of Education Richard Riley. I also received a Community Development Award from the South DeKalb Business Community.

Results:
- An average increase of 5–7 NCEs per year on the ITBS test.
- Parent volunteer hours increased from 50 hours in 1996 to more than 1,000 in 1997 and remained at that number until I left in 1999.
- PTA membership and attendance increased 100 percent.
- Parental involvement in other school functions increased 100 percent.
- Discipline referrals decreased each year to a minimum number.
- The percent of students completing and returning homework increased more than 80% year one.
- Vandalism decreased to zero.
- Parents transitioned from welfare to work.

Achievements:
- Recognition from President Clinton.
- John Stanford Hero Award: U.S. Department of Education.

- First school in DeKalb to partner with Georgia Partnership for Excellence in Education.
- Received Pay-for-Performance (Governor's Merit Pay).
- Received $50,000.00 from Gateway 2000.
- Three-year recipient of Next Generation Schools Grant.
- Received M. L. King Humanitarian Award.
- Numerous awards and cover stories in *The Atlanta Journal-Constitution*.

Community Development Model

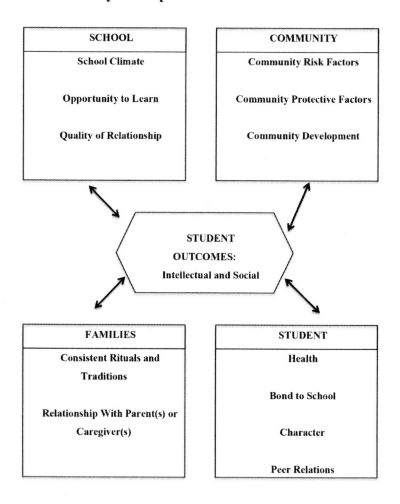

In 2000, I was appointed principal of Wynbrooke Elementary School in DeKalb County. At the time, Wynbrooke was a new school still under construction. Wynbrooke Traditional Theme School, as it was called, opened on January 8th, 2002. It's still operating today.

We opened this new school and developed the curriculum and school mission around the concept of a theme school that was focused on high academic achievement. The theme school program at Wynbrooke focused on students as active participants involved in research-centered assignments and hands-on projects in a highly structured interdisciplinary educational program. Special features of the theme school program included:

- Concentrated instruction in all core subjects.
- Emphasis on critical thinking and problem solving.
- Required parental involvement.
- Required student school/community involvement.
- Low pupil-teacher ratio.
- Foreign language instruction.
- Strict conduct code.
- Required uniforms and a strict dress code.
- Required daily homework.
- Tutorial program.
- "Agenda" planner required for all students.

Parents were a vital part of this program. The students wore uniforms, and contracts were established with parents concerning their role with assisting their children with reaching high levels of academic achievement as well as their volunteer service to the school.

We continued our focus on the community development and outreach by partnering with less fortunate schools in Niagara who became pen pals for students at Wynbrooke. This relationship resulted in more than $8,000 being raised to replace the roof on three schools. After two years at Wynbrooke, I was promoted to a central office position. During the 2004 school year, I served as executive director for special projects. In this position, I developed two projects:

- Dropout Roundup. Through a variety of outreach activities, high school dropouts were identified and redirected to either re-enroll in school or continue their education through the GED program.
- Project Achieve GED Program in partnership with DeKalb County Juvenile Judges. Working in collaboration with one of the state court judges in the DeKalb County Juvenile Court System, this program allowed juvenile defenders an opportunity to attend Project Achieve to receive their GED in lieu of jail time. The program has achieved significant results in eliminating incarceration for juvenile offenders who attended and successfully completed the program.

I was then promoted to assistant superintendent for school administration, where I had direct supervisory responsibility over thirty-five principals and the schools in which they were assigned. During my final year with the DeKalb School System, I served as associate superintendent for school administration. In this position, I had administrative oversight for all 158 schools/ centers and principals in the district.

I'm not providing this information because I'm trying to present myself as someone special. To the contrary, I'm just a typical public school principal like thousands of others across the country who cares deeply about their schools and their students. I happened to have had the opportunity to make a difference and, with the support of staff, community stakeholders, parents, and students, we were able to improve our schools and demonstrate that if you go beyond the schoolyard, you can get results.

Final Words

I hope this book has helped you understand the history of public school reform efforts and how we have too often responded to an event or perceived crisis with the urgent call to "do something" to "fix" our public schools. In reality, experience and studies have shown time and time again that America's public schools are more than capable of educating our children. America's public school system has never been broken, nor is it now.

We recognize that at schools in low-income neighborhoods, improvement is necessary. We have learned that if we want to improve student performance at school, we need to go beyond the schoolyard and into the community. When students arrive at school ready to learn and ready to profit from the school experience, we don't need Superman and we don't need billions in federal funds for "school improvement." What we need are public schools that are willing to embrace their communities, and political leaders who are willing to put our tax dollars where they will do the most good: where they can directly impact the lives of our fellow citizens who live without good jobs, without opportunities, and without resources, regardless of the color of their skin or their native language.

To make progress, we must identify leaders who understand that social context and effective planning are interdependent terms.

For each school, we must determine the gap between where the school is and where we want it to be, and then develop a plan with solutions identified to resolve the social issues that are contributing to the achievement gap.

We must correctly identify the problems, develop valid goals, and evaluate them frequently.

When a solution does not work, we must be willing to try another.

We must remember that problems are contextual, and there is no one-size-fits-all solution, nor is there a best practice that works in every case.

Thank you for reading this book. The next time you drive by one of America's public schools, think about what you can do to help the students in your community to succeed at school—and at life.